THE SUNFLOWER THAT BLOSSOMED THROUGH THE STORM

BY LASHONTA MCCRAY

THE SUNFLOWER THAT BLOSSOMED THROUGH THE STORM

A MEMOIR

ISBN: (979-8-218-34994-3)

by Lashonta McCray.

DEDICATED TO...

MARKEISHA CHARLES
PATSY MCCRAY
JOHN MCCRAY

TABLE OF CONTENTS:

Forward:
by Dapharoah69
Author of the Award-Winning, Bestselling Series "The King of Erotica"

Rarely do I endorse or help anyone when it comes to writing and publishing books, especially after doing this for 24 years. Not because I couldn't, but because I've been burned by opportunists along this literary journey. It can be daunting and tiring. Not to be discouraged, I matured, and that mindset changed. One bad apple shouldn't spoil the bunch.

Since then, I've helped a few authors bring their dream of a published book to life free of charge, and in that I became of service; service that wasn't available to me when I started my writing journey.

Twenty-four years ago, no one helped me publish my work. I solicited other authors, but I was ignored, or my emails were sent to the spam folder. I was homeless and alone. I was eating out of garbage cans for food. I was broke, broken and alone.

In fact, when I informed my family that I was writing a book, they laughed in my face and said that I wasn't "smart enough" to write one, neither did they know that I was homeless. I was called everything, but a child of God.

In silence, I remember my best friend bought me a laptop and I wrote my first book for publishing in five days, from a sleeping bag in the bushes on what is now the Homestead Air Reserve Park. Around that time, it hadn't a name, and the patch of land filled with trees was just ashes left from the effects of Hurricane Andrew in 1992.

I wrote a 600 page book called *"The King of Erotica book 1: The Throne."* I used to cry myself to sleep, hoping and praying that my book would come out.

Publisher after publisher said "no," or that I was talented, but my stories were too black, too this, or too that. I published my stories online. I hired an editor in the industry that polished my book, and I re-released it with a new cover.

Unfortunately, my book was filled with errors, and I discovered that he didn't edit anything. He pretended to do the work and ran off with two thousand dollars of my money, money that took me a year to save. I tried to commit suicide, but I couldn't bring myself to do it.

Somehow, those errors fueled the raunchy characters in my book and over a year it became a Barnes and Noble.com Top 100 Bestseller from word of mouth alone.

I prayed to God and did it on my own. Three weeks after my first book release, I met Lashonta McCray in Naranja through a mutual friend.

From hello, I loved her. She was humble, giving and painfully real. Looking into her eyes, it felt like I had known her all my life. She has one of the biggest hearts I'd ever encountered.

We understood each other. We just clicked. I never met a woman I embraced from the gate.

We became good friends, and we bonded into brother and sister over the past two decades. She's family.

My family adores her, from my spouse to my siblings. She not only became my sister, but she has been there for me during the good and the bad. Through my darkest hours, she cried with me, gave me a place of peace, and comforted me.

She mentioned that she wanted me to help her write a book over ten years ago, but our busy lives pulled us in two different directions.

Then, last year, Lashonta called me and said that she was ready to tell her story. I told her what was needed, and she jumped on it, no questions asked. She is the only debut author I helped that did what was required, and the first page wasn't written yet.

She bought a tape recorder, and we met up countless times and I pressed record. I sat by her side as she began her testimony that had us both on an emotional rollercoaster.

Over the coming months, I would sit in the car and type up hours of recordings, something I have never done for anybody, ever, into the book you now read.

Formatting it was daunting. I had to relive her grief, her anguish, and her pain. I had to deal with two deaths in my family and relive my own experiences as an abused kid. Nonetheless, this isn't about me, it is about my sister and her testimony, told in her own voice.

Presenting "The Sunflower That Blossomed Through The Storm" is a complete blessing, and an honor.

I feel like God allowed me to go through the downside of publishing and brought me through my own struggles, so I could show someone else how to avoid the middleman and become their own publisher. To control their own narrative.

I highly recommend "The Sunflower That Blossomed Through The Storm" to anyone that has ever loved, to anyone that has ever lived a life of success and failure, to anyone that have been abused.

This is for the young mothers and the irresponsible young men that need guidance from a resilient woman that didn't let abuse or the streets define her.

I recommend this book to the younger women on their journey to adulthood. I recommend this book to my nieces and nephews.

Lashonta is not only a victor and a survivor, but she is also a woman that embraces who she is. She doesn't edit or compromise her integrity, her testimony or those she love for anything.

As a young teenage mother, she defied the odds and raised her daughter, whom I love dearly, into a successful, productive woman that is happily married with young daughters of her own.

I remember every talk Lashonta and I ever had. I remember visiting her in the hospital years ago when I found out she was there, and like the goof-balls we were, I did everything that I could to make her laugh and smile.

Lashonta has given me a shoulder to cry on numerous times without shame or ridicule.

I've given my shoulder in return, for her to use anytime she needs to. During the creation of her memoirs, she cooked for me, my spouse, and my mom and made sure that I was good. She made sure I had my favorite snacks and something in my pocket, and I didn't ask her for it. She opened her home to me and provided a quiet, safe environment. Again, this shows just how beautiful her heart is.

I am proud to be of service to someone outside of myself. God gave me the gift and the success to be a blessing to others.

At times this book almost didn't come to be because of the traumatic events that occurred in my life during this book's creation, but I could never give up on someone else's dream because of obstacles.

For the young woman or young man that read this book, may Lashonta's testimony be a bridge between right and wrong.

May her testimony serve as a U-Turn sign for those that want to live the street life. May this testimony teach young men how to respect women and their minds, hearts, and bodies.

Most importantly, may Lashonta's testimony heal her wounds, and be a roadmap to forgiving herself for all she has gone through.

She came out on top, as not only a Queen, but also as a resilient mother, an amazing grandmother, and a loyal sister. She is more of a sister to me than my blood sister. I put my heart and my energy into this as if it was my own.

I wish Lashonta nothing but the best, blessings, and success. I am so very proud of her, for overcoming obstacles, for defying the odds, for remaining humble, loving, and resilient.

For showing us all how to smell *the Sunflower That Blossomed Through the Storm*. And that smell broke her generational curse.

With love, honor, and respect to a Queen.
Dapharoah69

THE SUNFLOWER THAT BLOSSOMED THROUGH THE STORM

LOVE

Love is supposed to be beautiful,
Yet it can hurt so much
You lose your thoughts
On where to go
Or forget what to do
Love feels like a cold drink
Down your throat
On a hot, summer day
Or a full massage with oil
Caressed all over your body
By the hands of the one
You lust for
It can also feel sadness,
like you're grieving a loved one
Your heart is about to explode
It beats out of your chest
But you still let him come

Upload himself in you
Yet your heart is broken
He doesn't see you
For the exceptional woman
that you are
You deserve better
Life is so much greater
So run, my child
And don't look back
There's so much more to life,
than forgetting where to go
Or what to do

<u>LASHONTA MCCRAY</u>

<u>Acknowledgements</u>

My story come in blood raw fashion. If you're
triggered by abuse, mental illness, assault, drugs,
depression, and death then maybe this isn't for you.

Lashonta McCray

INTRODUCTION

Greetings, dear reader. My name is Lashonta McCray. You may or may not know me, maybe you have heard about me, but I appreciate your time, your company, and your energy. I'm sure you have other things to do and more important places to be.

With great regards, I present to you, my memoirs. I share my testimony on these pages in sound heart, mind, body and soul. My intentions are non-malicious.

I do this as part of a legacy I want to inevitably pass down to my daughter and my beautiful grandchildren.

My story come in blood raw fashion. If you're triggered by abuse, mental illness, assault, drugs, depression, and death then maybe this isn't for you.

I'm telling you the triggers ahead of time, so this will be your only warning.

I must warn you that my life wasn't filled with fairy-tale happy endings, white picket fences or knights in shining armor sweeping me off my feet.

While you're here, I'll delve into the reasons why I'm thankful that I'm in the position to give my testimony, and why I'm grateful to God for allowing me to tell it from my lips to these pages.

I'm a Christian. I believe in God, yet I'm not a saint. I'm not perfect.

I have a big heart that's filled with love, hurt, pain and turmoil. The wounds may have healed, but the scars remain. I'm a work in progress.

I have my good and bad days, and I face my fears. I sin, I have flaws, and sometimes the rain outshines the sun.

We all have a story to tell, but I control my narrative.

My been-through strengthened me into the strong woman I've become. I've endured sexual abuse, prostitution, scams, fraud, robbing and selling drugs.

I've been a fool in love that was blinded by money and lust.

I've grieved traumatic losses. I was a naïve, misled teenage mother that found her own way when I was hustling in the cold streets of Opa-Locka, Florida (Miami).

I also helped raise my siblings to the best of my ability. I want to be a shining example to my daughter and my grandchildren that life isn't just a dream.

My story will detail what it looks like to rise and fall and rise again in the face of adversity, bad relationships and oppression.

The purpose of "The Sunflower That Blossomed Through the Storm" is to inspire young girls, young ladies, young women and young mothers-to-be, to become their greatest selves, but that comes with obstacles and devastating losses.

My successes and failures serve as a blueprint to show teenage girls, young mothers, and promiscuous young women how to carry themselves from ladies to Queens without compromising their self-respect or their dignity.

I'll show, through my own predicaments, how to love your body enough to protect it and safety at all costs.

This is also for the young men that refuse to be good fathers, the young men that are in the streets gang banging, and the men that foolishly breaks a woman's heart.

I had to deal with a lot of dysfunctional circumstances and trauma in my life in ways that nearly broke me as a child.

If this testimony can help one person, it'll make a difference to me.

The purpose of telling my story is simple. A lot of people that know me, don't know me.

As an adolescent growing up in Opa-Locka, I always had a mean expression or a frown on my face, like I didn't want to be bothered.

I was deeply hurt on the inside.

I experienced a lot of pain. I truly, from my heart, want readers to know what I really went through.

I want family, friends and those who don't know me to understand my struggles. For a long time, they've been outside, looking in.

I want them to read about what I went through, and how I survived it as a victor, not a victim.

In five years, I see myself being a homeowner. I already fixed my credit. My beautiful daughter has been repairing people's credit for the past three years, so credit is not a problem.

Right now, I'm learning how to save money. I have a spending habit.

Owning a home is a dream of mine so my grandkids can come to a place of love.

I want to leave them a legacy they can be proud of. It was something my grandparents did for me and my siblings.

My mother and father never reciprocated the gesture, or the generation after them.

Unfortunately, my big brother Vare lost the house my great-grandparents had for nearly fifty years, which I will get into later in the book. It was heartbreaking. He lost the only home me and my siblings had to go to.

When it came to my mother's drug abuse problem, if she had received the proper help, it would have broken a cycle of dysfunction in my family, but that help never came, and that cycle was never broken.

Some things were meant to be.

I truly apologize for all of my transgressions and bad judgement.

I was reckless and selfish in my earlier days.

Again, this may anger some, enrage a few, or make you sad.

Maybe it won't, but this is bigger than emotion and redemption.

My feelings, spirit and good heart was broken for decades, leading to this testimony.

I accept and acknowledge my wrong-doing.

I forgave myself and found peace within my being.

I chose to be a responsible mother and grandmother, sister, and a friend.

I let go and let God.

In retrospection, it doesn't make me feel good about the things I've done.

With my autobiography, my intimate memoirs, I will destroy the generational curse and break the cycle of dysfunction that nearly destroyed me.

Most importantly, it is my wish that my life inspires my daughter and grandchildren to become something even greater than me.

Moreover, may I inspire the teenage mother
that doesn't see the end in sight, or the young man
loading his pistol to rob someone so he can eat.
It leads to jail or the grave.
Hey, young world.
You are enough.

Sincerely,
Lashonta McCray

PRELUDE:

In a stolen car, Al, Nard and Dan were cruising through an area by Opa-Locka, driving pretty fast. I was watching from the backseat. Two dudes were walking, talking, and minding their business in the middle of the street, not too far from Bunch Park. We were headed back to the Miami Inn.

Frustrated, Al started blowing the horn, hoping they would move out of the way.

Honk! Honk!

"Get y'all asses outta the road!"

Defensively, Al guided the car to the left a bit to keep from hitting them. They flipped their middle fingers at us, talking shit like they were about that life.

They had no idea that we were a bunch of rebellious teens who did not give a fuck about nothing in life in that moment.

Al frowned. "I know those fuck niggas ain't talking shit!"

Before Al could stop the car, Dan opened the back door. He was on the back seat with me.

"What you said nah, fuck nigga?"

One of the dudes said, "Don't worry 'bout it muthafuckah!"

"These niggas still talking shit? I should shoot your fuck ass!"

"That's right pussy ass niggas. Buss his ass, brother," I yelled from the car.

Narrowing his eyes, Dan shot at them....

One of the dude's shirts began turning red....

THE SUNFLOWER THAT BLOSSOMED THROUGH THE STORM

Chapter One:
Childhood Memories

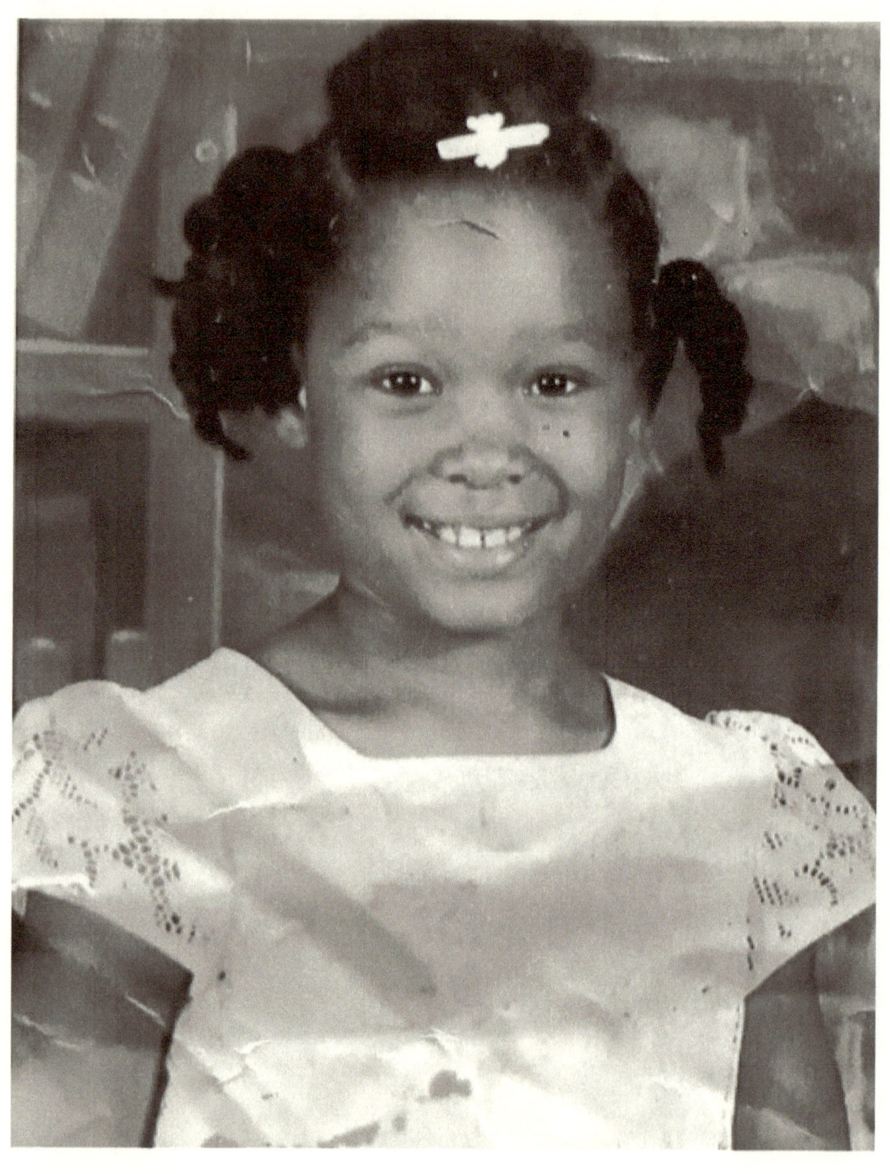

I was born at Jackson Memorial Hospital on Saturday, April 8,1978. I was raised in Opa Locka, Florida, a sub-division of Miami-Dade County. I was brought up by my loving great grandparents (on my mom Charlotte's side). My great-grandfather, John Henry McCray, was born in 1909 and my great grandma, Patsy McCray, was born in 1914.

They were raised during a time when a lot of secrets were kept, and a lot of things were covered up.

The earliest I can remember is being five years old. I remember the simple things, like my great-grandfather John making Sunday dinners. He would cook smothered fried chicken with grits.

He always bought a gallon of lemon drink. I affectionately called him Pa-pa. He worked all the time. All he knew was work, work, work.

Unfortunately, he didn't know his family. He didn't know where he came from, but he did make his own family with his wife.

I didn't know where the name "McCray" originated from in our family; neither did he. To my understanding, he was adopted into the name "McCray."

He had siblings he never saw, knew about, or met. He did find one of his sister's daughters, his niece. And she had kids, but they didn't have "McCray" for a last name. They were from his bloodline.

I never knew "McCray" was my Pa-Pa's adopted name until my great-grandma Patsy told me. I looked forward to Sunday dinners. They brought me so much joy. He was family-oriented, but he was a Player.

My great-grandma Patsy told me that she gave her life to Christ when she was thirty-six years old. She instantly stopped sleeping with my great-granddaddy.

As the events unfolded between them, Mama would tell all their dirt out of anger because she couldn't get money for her crack habit.

She would blurt it out to my great-grandma Patsy what Pa-Pa was doing with her friends in the streets that were her age, women she went to school with, that were also doing drugs.

One of the women was named Allison. My Pa-Pa used to have sex with her. Mama would throw it in my great-grandma's face.

My great-grandma was such a lady, such a class act, that she didn't entertain Mama's foolishness.

She ignored it all together, and kept going about her merry way. If Mama thought great-grandma was going to fold and give her money for crack, then she was mistaken.

Great-grandma Patsy told me one time, "I know about your Pa-Pa. Nobody is perfect. Your

Pa-Pa has a son out there. One lady came to my gate one time, with a little boy at her side, saying that he was Pa-Pa's son. Pa-pa ran them away."

And she never saw them again. She knew what he was doing, but he was her husband and she stuck by him, no matter what.

He made sure the bills were paid. He made sure that everybody was taken care of, then he did his thing afterwards. He eventually gave his life to Christ when he was eighty years old.

He found out that he had prostate gland cancer, and he only had so long to live. He was scared to die. Around this time, he wasn't running the streets. He worked and came home.

He died a few months after the surgery.

From as early as five years old, I remember our conversations. As a little girl I never understood why Pa-pa taught me the importance of making my own money.

With a stern voice, he would tell me, "Don't let anybody take advantage of you!"

He was preparing me for the world. It gave me a sense of comfort knowing that he cared. He didn't have those talks with anybody else but me.

I remember when he took me to the Pussy Cat Club, a strip joint that was by the Miami International Airport. There was a naked neon lady sign above it. You could see it from the Turnpike.

In the parking lot, I used to sit in a white station wagon, and I would see the naked strippers going in and out of the place. Pa-Pa regularly met his boss man at the club. His boss used to drive a Corvette. I fell in love with Corvettes at that moment.

I didn't have a male role model in my life. My dad was in prison most of my life, so my great-grandfather and I were attached because of it.

My mom, Charlotte, never knew her dad. My great grandparents (Charlotte's grandparents) raised her.

Her mother was a teenage mom. My grandmother, Lollipop (my mother's mother), never claimed me or my siblings. I really didn't know my grandmother Lollipop, but that was another story.

I remember when Mama never really spent quality time with me or my siblings, but when she did, we used to watch *Gilligan's Island* on a small black and white TV.

One time she laid me in front of her when she was pregnant with my baby sister, Gin.

Gin was named after a character on *Gilligan's Island.* That one moment with Mama was special to me. Believe it or not it made me feel loved and wanted. I had so much joy. She was embracing me, showing genuine affection.

My father was incarcerated at the time. That was my first time having knowledge of him going to prison.

As a child I was isolated. I didn't really come out of my shell until I was eleven years old. I was an introvert. I didn't speak a lot. I was somewhat quiet and to myself.

I observed a lot of things. It was easy for me to shut down at that age.

I remember another time, around Christmas, Mama bought me and my sister big wheels. Considering she never really bought us stuff, this was major.

I wasn't raised in my great grandparent's house until the age of five.

My sister and I used to ride our big wheels around our neighborhood, the entire complex.

We were happy and excited to ride our new toys.

We had such joy riding around seeing everybody. We focused on having a good time. I loved bonding with my sibling. We didn't have any worries.

As I grew older, I realized how my mother bought our big wheels.

I remember when my parents lived together. It was my mom, my dad, my little brother Dave, me, and my baby sister Tie.

Altogether my mom would have five kids, my last sibling wasn't my dad's kid.

All my parents did was fight. That was not a good example for me or my siblings.

Part of me feels like maybe the wrong type of seeds were planted in our minds.

Truth be told, I didn't remember any happy moments when me and my siblings lived with my parents before I turned five years old.

Mama was beautiful, light skinned, had a head full of hair and stood about 5 foot 6. My dad was about 5 foot 7. Mama had her last child when my dad went to prison for armed robbery. I was close to six years old. The early 80s.

My dad and two other dudes robbed a random place. An unknown victim was hurt badly by my dad and two thugs. Yes, they had guns.

To my understanding there were two versions of the story. The first story I heard was that my mom grabbed us from our apartment and took us to my great grandparents' house.

The police were everywhere, flashing lights and sirens blared in front of the house. Me and my siblings were crying. We were traumatized and scared.

We really didn't know what was going on. My siblings were cutting up, wanting answers. Mama told us to be quiet.

I asked anyway. "Mama, what's going on?"

That's when I found out dad went to jail for robbery.

This was also the first time I was separated from my father.

CHAPTER TWO:
NATIONALITY

I was isolated growing up. I didn't come out of my shell until I was eleven, going on twelve years old. I was slow to speak. I observed a lot of things. It was easy for me to shut down.

I remember the Early 80s Opa-Locka. My great grandma was a Christian. She was one of those women that didn't play the radio. Patsy McCray. She was married twice.

She was quick to say, "Shut cha mouff....! *Stay outta my business!*"

My great grandma's mama was mixed with white, black, and Native American.

Her skin wasn't mixed right. Her hands leading up to her elbows was white. Up further was black. Her face was white; her neck was black. Her mother looked the same way.

Her mother's dad was white. And her mother was Cherokee Indian. My mom was high yellow due to our genetics.

My skin tone was like pecan. I was considered dark when it came to my siblings and Mama. I was actually my dad's complexion and his mom.

My daddy spoiled me. I got away with everything, and I didn't know if I loved it or not.

I was daddy's little girl. I got away with stealing his cars when I was ten, eleven years old.

He was just released from prison around that time.

He was letting me get away with murder, figuratively speaking. I would take his keys and steal the car and joy ride with my friends, having the time of my life. Being fearless was the thing to do.

I wasn't nervous because it was daddy. I was good for it, at least that was what I thought. I didn't think of the principle of my wrongdoing because in my mind principles were opportunities.

Basically, I was doing what I wanted to do. He never spanked me; he never beat me; he never abused me.

I was grateful for that. In my 'hood you had fathers battling their own demons, yet all black fathers didn't beat their kids or take out their failures and shortcomings on them.

My dad was one of those selfless men. And I loved him for that. The only thing he would really say to me was, "Sugar, you know you're wrong."

That's all, that's it. No two-week punishments, no screaming, and no abuse.

He didn't yell; he didn't curse. He didn't say things that brought me down; he didn't say things that hurt my self-confidence.

He didn't say things that was disrespectful. He didn't do any of that.

I remember before he went to prison, he told me and my siblings to form a line so he could spank us one at a time.

We were on the back porch. He put me on his knee, popped me once. It wasn't even hard.

"Don't do that no'mo," he said.

That was the extent of his discipline.

I would start laughing as I walked off.

In comparison to my dad, my mother was a character. I remembered when she started abusing me at the age of six years old.

I never knew why because at that age, you know, I was innocent. I was scared. I didn't like fights or confrontations. I didn't like to fuss; I didn't like to argue.

Before dad went to prison, he and Mama fought like cats and dogs. I never understood why Mama continued to have kids. I thought about it over the years, especially in the era when some women thought it was cool to have children from different men.

The streets talked badly about women like that. I learned that Mama only had kids with one man because she didn't want to embarrass herself or the family by having them from different men.

So, she had kids from the same man.

After birthing four kids, after all the arguing and the fights and whatever, she was the one that turned him in to the police when he did the robbery.

He would have gotten away, but Mama claimed that she didn't want that negativity around her kids, so she called the police and gave him up. I was in no position to oppose.

"Um, 911, yea, my husband did it. Come and pick his ass up!"

And just like that daddy was gone.

Mom felt like she had to turn him in for her to let him go and move on with her life.

Moved right on to a pregnancy from another sorry ass nigga, my lil sister's daddy, Gin, her fifth child (named after a character on Gilligan's Island).

Chapter Three:
Mama

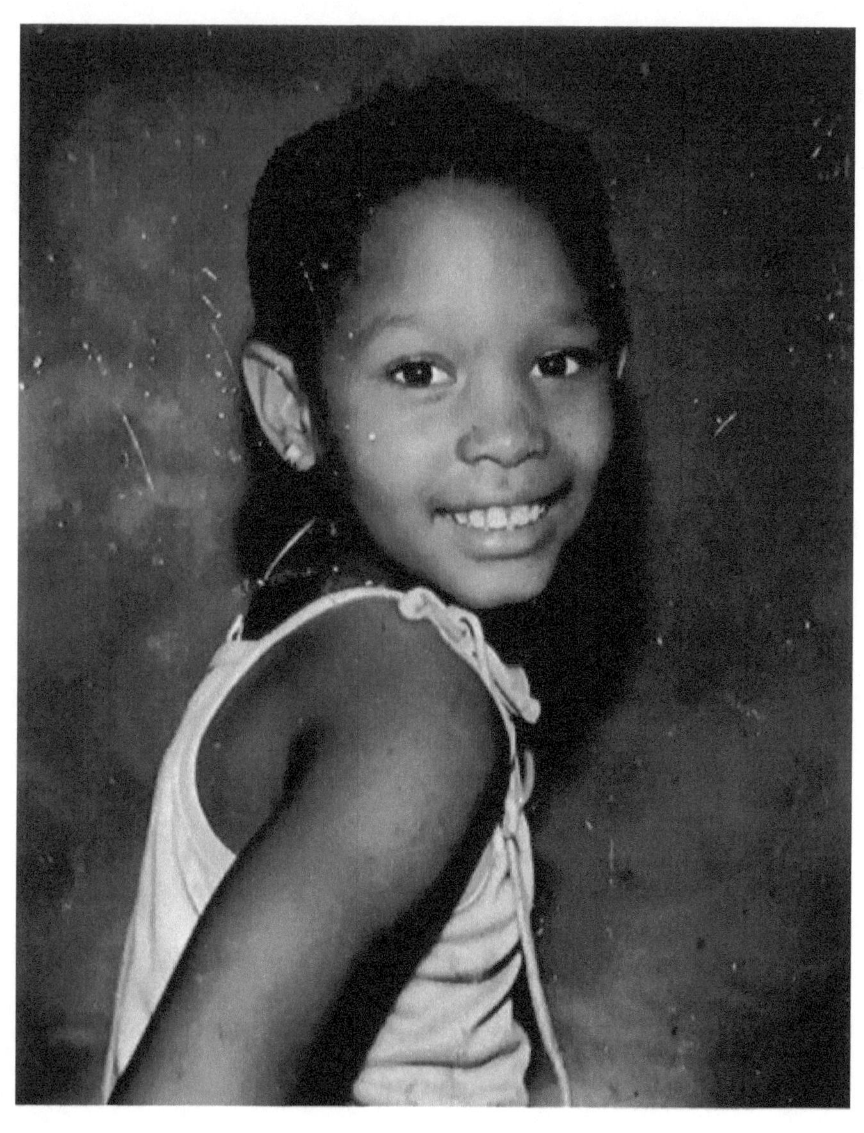

THE DEVIL

When she walked in the room,
the frown on her face...
I know once she heard the word "no,"
she was going to turn into a devil.
The devil that I was scared of,
the devil that abused me,
the devil that neglected me,
the devil that hurt me,
the devil that I couldn't get away from:
that Devil was my Mama.
All I wanted her to do is hug me, love me,
talk to me and embrace me...
but yeah, she did the opposite.
She hit me, cursed me, snatched my hair out,
and cracked my teeth.
Yes! I love her, my mom...
That's who was supposed to protect me, teach me,
And love me, but she didn't...
Do you know why?
Because her mom didn't do it for her,
my grandma, who don't love her,

me or my siblings.
I'm lost....
Her mom received love from both parents,
yet she was the first devil towards my mom.
I blame her, the Devil's mom, my grandma,
the woman that didn't love us.
How can you live with yourself,
knowing you have five grandkids...
That you never tried to love.

Lashonta McCray

I had the type of mother that wasn't nurturing, never styled my hair, never helped me with my homework, and never took me to a doctor's appointment. She never took me to the dentist. There was never any hugs and kisses.

I didn't have that type of mother. I tried to speak to her over time, but she constantly told me to get over it, that my trauma was old, that she didn't remember.

Now that she was saved, she admitted that a lot of things she didn't remember. At the end of the day, she left permanent scars on her kids. Every last one of us had some type of resentment towards her. I wasn't saying that I didn't love her, but the traumatic things she put us through, and her lack of good parenting followed us into adulthood.

A lot of my siblings still point the finger at her because of their downfall and bad decision making. I didn't think that was fair because I was the only one that was abused out of all five of her kids. My mom was a light-skinned woman.

My siblings were also light skinned. I was the darkest one out of the bunch.

I had more of a pecan complexion. I used to cry about my color. I felt so different. That's just the tip of the iceberg about why I felt that way.

Most of my immediate family and my mom had lighter skin.

I wasn't really dark skinned, but in comparison to my family, I was. I was more of my dad's color, and his mom, and his side of the family. That was also a problem for me as a child.

I remember we stayed in the apartments behind Ali Baba Bar off of NW 27th Avenue in Opa-Locka.

One day my Pa-Pa came over to our house. He knocked on the door. I was sitting on the floor, and Mama was sitting on the couch eating a runny egg.

I didn't know what a sunny side up egg was. All I knew was that they looked crazy. I was a real picky eater.

Pa-Pa came inside the house. "Charlotte! You should know better," he scolded. "You have soiled diapers everywhere, leading all the way up to your door, and down the hallway. You know the smell from the pampers is coming from your house. That's just nasty! Look at the dirty dishes! You need to get up and do better."

I remember him saying that. In that same apartment, I was awakened in the middle of the night from my baby brother Dave crying. He was in a shitty diaper, and it was running over with boo boo and pee.

I was five years old. I didn't think I started school yet because I had no memories of school before that. My brother was in a pamper and he couldn't walk. I was older than him. He was around the crawling stage. My sister Tie was about three years old.

I held him while he was hollering and screaming. I looked around the apartment for Mama. Tie followed behind me, but she wasn't crying. I didn't know what to do with him. He dangled from my arms.

There were sliding glass doors behind our apartment that faced the Arab liquor bar. We sat on the floor by the glass doors. I knew Mama had to be at the bar because she used to be over there all the time.

There was a man in a wheelchair, Mama's friend that used to come by. He'd tell me, "I'll buy you some potato chips if you roll me to the liquor store."

I pushed him there in his wheelchair, he'd buy me the chips, and I'd roll him back home.

I knew that was a place Mama hung out at, so I sat by the sliding glass doors with my baby brother and my little sister and waited on my her.

I didn't recall her coming home that night. Maybe because we fell asleep. To wake up with my baby brother (that couldn't walk, soiled in a pamper I didn't know how to change), screaming at the top of his lungs, was a traumatic experience.

My little sister was there with us.

Our oldest brother never lived with us, so he wasn't there. I was really scared.

After my daddy went to jail, I started living at my great-grandma's house. Mama was angry and bitter. As a result, she fussed at great-grandma Patsy all the time for money. And when great grandma didn't give her the money, Mama started beating on me.

"Do you know how much I hate you?"

"Your skin color is ugly!"

"I found you under a garbage can!"

I used to ask myself why my Pa-Pa and great grandma wouldn't make her stop assaulting me mentally, physically, and emotionally.

They fussed and threatened her, but they never called the police, they didn't jump in the middle of her beating me, nor did they stop it.

I felt unwanted because...what 6 or 7 year old was beaten with extension cords?

My great grandma wouldn't give her money for crack, so she beat me with the black extension cord attached to the little gray Nintendo controller. My big brother had a Nintendo, so I remember.

I remember another time my great grandma wouldn't give her money for crack.

My great grandma's curtains used to drape the windows from a wooden rod.

The wooden rod wasn't too thick, and it wasn't too thin. She beat me with that wooden rod.

That was something I buried in the back of my mind, and I didn't talk about it.

I wondered why Mama, when she couldn't get money for drugs from my great grandma, would immediately start beating on me.

She didn't just brutally assault me, she abused me with extension cords of all kinds, the one you plug in the wall and the one attached to the video game controller and wooden rods.

From age six to ten years old I suffered that magnitude of abuse. That lady tortured me for many years!

This lady fucking beat on me because she couldn't get high on great grandma's dime.

No, it didn't happen every day, but she handed out random beatings with objects.

She constantly reminded me of my ugly skin color. How she didn't like me.

"When you was a baby, you was an ugly, whining child! You whined like a fucking cat!" she said maliciously.

"I'm embarrassed to tote you because you're so fucking ugly! And your daddy used to trail behind me, with your ugly, pointed eared ass! I can't stand your ass!"

Those were Mama's exact words. Parents needed to be careful about what they said to kids because some of those words clung to them and followed them into adulthood. Some of those things fucked with them mentally.

Some of those things may make them evil and angry. Some of the things you tell them might cause them to hurt other people.

They can become suicidal or cause them to feel worthless.

Parents should understand that what they went through in life should not be subjected to their children.

CHAPTER FOUR: THE DEVIL

My grandma Lily (my dad's mom) and Pa-Pa tried their best to **raise** me between two households. Grandma Lily knew what Mama was doing to me. I was the only child out of five living between two households.

Mama snatched my hair out from the root, she cracked my teeth, and I ran away. And when she caught me, she beat me even worse, like she didn't give a fuck.

She damaged and abused me any way she could. She even started abusing me in the street in front of people.

As a child, I was like damn, when I was in the house she beat me, when I was outside, she beat me, if I was out of her sight, she'd run me down and beat me.

I couldn't get away from that monster. I hated her! *I hated her!* Why did she have to have me?

Why did she have to be my Mama?

Why was my skin so ugly?

Why were my ears so pointy?

Why was I so different?

Was that why she didn't love me, because I was different? Was that why she always talked bad about my skin color? Was it because I favored my Daddy's side of the family? She always threw that in my face.

Why didn't she love me? I always questioned myself as a child. Why?

Mama would say, "I can't stand you! You look like your grandma Lily! You favor them! You act like them on your Daddy's side…" Na, na, na!

She always compared me to my dad and my grandma Lily. She constantly reminded me that she couldn't stand them, and she couldn't stand me.

On top of that, when I was in the fourth or fifth grade, I was taken out of school sometimes just to go with my great grandma to take care of her business because she couldn't read.

Even though Mama tortured me physically and mentally, I was an A+ student.

I was very intelligent. I was very bright when it came to my education. I wasn't going to lie, what gave me the urge to not want to be in school, was because I was continuously taken out of school to help my great grandma.

For example, I was taken out of school to go with her to the welfare office, when she had to recertify.

I literally knew all of my siblings, and first cousins, birthdays and Social Security numbers by heart.

I sat by great grandma Patsy, and the case worker would ask, "Okay, what's this person's birthday and Social Security number?" and I would tell her from memory.

"What's the birthday?"

And I'd tell her.

"What's the social security number?'

And I'd tell her.

"Next!"

I'd tell her.

"Next!"

I'd tell her. For all parties on the list. I was programmed. Mama had five kids, and my auntie Aretha had three kids.

I knew all their birthdays and Social Security numbers by heart, for all eight of us.

Plus, my great grandma Patsy was a foster parent and ran a shelter home. So, when my great-grandma Patsy got all of us, the state took her license because they said she didn't have enough room for more kids.

She adopted a set of brothers, so that was two heads, Mama's five, Auntie Aretha's three, and her two oldest adopted kids.

They were older than all of the other kids. They were living there before all of us, so that was eight, nine, and ten heads.

My Mama was number eleven, my Auntie
Aretha was number twelve. My Pa-Pa and great
grandma was number thirteen and fourteen.

It was fourteen of us living in a two bedroom
house until my Pa-Pa built additions to the house.
He built a living room, and another room. It was
now a three bedroom house with a kitchen and
dining room.

Unfortunately, Mama was such a bully. Auntie
Aretha was always bullied by her. Out of Grandma
Lollipop's kids, it was my Mama, my Auntie
Aretha, then she had my mom's brother.
Mama never knew her dad. I didn't know who my
granddaddy was on either side of the family.
I only have one granddaddy I had my whole life,
and that was my great-granddaddy, my Pa-Pa.

I remember I went to Mama's place. She had a
boyfriend named Lepo. They lived in a Room-
in house on Ali Baba. I didn't care how badly
Mama treated me, I still had love for her.

I just hated the way she abused me.

There was a difference.

I had to go across the tracks, State Road 9, and
all those busy roads as a little girl at nine and ten
years old just to see her.

If anybody from Opa-Locka knew about State
Road 9, you'd know what I was talking about.

I had to walk through Segal Park, cut through the neighborhood, go through the cuts in the gate and cross those busy highways.

I walked across the railroad tracks and her duplex was right there in front of me.

When I entered Mama's place, my auntie was there.

Mama was arguing with her. "I found your panties in my motherfucking room!" Mama said with a nasty tone. "I know you're not fucking my man, bitch! I know you're not fucking my man!"

I was like, uh-huh.

What the fuck is going on? Auntie is messing with...no, I don't think so!

That was all I could recall. I remember a fist fight at that moment.

Another time, I was at my great grandma's house. Mama swung at my auntie, and they started fighting in the bathroom.

I went in there, too and the door closed.

"Fight her back, auntie!" I shouted. "Auntie, fight her back!"

My auntie flipped Mama in the tub, boom! And she whipped Mama's ass.

Whoop!

Whoop!

Whoop!

Whoop!

Whoop!

I cheered my auntie on.

Finally, my Auntie fought back.

Mama didn't just beat on me she beat on my auntie as well. She was just a fucking bully.

Even out in the streets I used to hear about her fighting people.

The woman was a nasty bully.

I didn't understand or have knowledge of drugs back then. Especially at that age. It was also confusing. My mother used to fuss at my great-grandparents because she wanted money. And she'd take it out on me if she couldn't get it. She was a dope fiend mother. I had a dope fiend daddy.

Well, I took that back. My dad wasn't a dope fiend. I called Mama a dope fiend because she let crack overpower her ability to be a good mother.

That went up in smoke every time she got high.

Chapter Five:
The Streets

The decisions Mama made in the streets affected me as a child. I endured community gossip about Mama.

It was embarrassing and painful to hear random stories about Mama's affairs from strangers in the streets.

The streets were disloyal. I mean people weren't exactly always speaking negatively about her, but her drug lifestyle was nothing good to hear about.

I was hanging out with my friends Tiny and Wanna at the apartments on 22nd Avenue by the light on 143rd Street.

They said they heard somebody moaning behind their bedroom window. Wanna said that she saw them in the act when she went to the bathroom to go pee.

They said some dude was fucking my Mama.
That was some horrific, terrorizing, and
traumatizing shit to hear.

I didn't know how true it was, but it hurts to
hear about it.

One day Mama looked at me and said, "I can't
stand you! You look like your daddy. I found you
in the garbage can!"

She told me that she found me in the garbage
can so much that I literally, as I grew up, thought
that I was born in the garbage can.

Psychologically, it affected me mentally and
emotionally. Especially coming from the woman
that gave me life.

How any mother could say that to her child
was beyond me anyway.

I couldn't wrap my mind around it. I really
didn't understand why it was going on and why she
was taking out her anger and frustrations on me. I
did absolutely nothing to harm my mother or hurt
her.

While my mother was abusing me, and saying
those hideous things to me, breaking my heart and
my spirit, my siblings and my cousins used to sit
back and laugh at me. Poke fun at me.

They found it entertaining. It hurt me deeply,
causing me to become more of an introvert
because my own siblings didn't comfort me.

I looked different; I looked a different color
than anyone else. I shook with tears as I thought
about it. I felt like I wasn't normal.

I loved my siblings and would protect them. I considered them to be my kids.

I took them to Open House and PTA meetings when I was eight, nine years old. Our school was four blocks down from my great-grandparents' house.

My great-grandma Patsy never knew how to read. She was born back in the slavery days when they were hidden in the back wooded areas, out of sight, out of view.

When black folks were condemned to the woods. Or when they were restricted to slave quarters. Or cabins you never saw in passing.

My great-grandmother Patsy was a slave. She cleaned white folks' houses. She even breast fed Caucasian babies.

I heard so many stories about those white folk she told me about, and none of it was good, but she taught me not to be racist.

When it came to the things going on around me, compared to the things my great-grandma had to painfully endure as a slave, I had no room to complain.

My great-grandma used to eat clay dirt because she barely had food from her master. When she gave birth, she was accompanied by a midwife because there weren't hospitals back then. Her nipple was cut off without pain meds because the milk in her breast spoiled. Pain meds didn't exist back then.

I could get deep into those stories.

Despite her painful past, she always taught me how to honor myself. She taught me how to respect myself.

If you borrowed money from anybody you made sure you paid it back in a timely fashion.

They shouldn't have to hunt you down for their money considering you didn't have to hunt them down to borrow it. Anybody could tell you that if I borrowed anything I paid it back.

It was about integrity with me. I wouldn't feel right as a woman if I didn't. I didn't care what I did in the streets, I never messed with cousins, brothers, or friends. I always respected myself and respected them.

Wherever I went people respected me. I loved to fight, never ran from a nigga or a bitch.

My daddy was a black belt. He learned it in prison on an expert level. He taught me how to subdue an opponent with certain moves.

My big brother taught me how to box. I wasn't your average female fighter. I could wrestle, shoot...I could do all that shit.

While in school I loved music, so I took a music class. I played the, um, I didn't remember the name of the instrument, but you blew in a piano-looking thing.

A melodica, probably. It was fun until I had to learn all those notes. Then I quit. I had to pass on that one. Suddenly, I didn't like music anymore.

Since my great-grandparents forced me to be in music class, I found something else.

I was also forced to be in the church choir by my great-grandparents.

We had to go to church every other day, and three different times on Sundays.

We attended Church of God by Faith in Opa-Locka located on 22nd Ave, right past NW 150th something.

It was a small, quaint-looking church. The Arab store, dubbed "the Mr. Beal store," was on the lefthand side of the street. Illegal business transactions took place there, and the dope peddling.

On the right side was Bobby Liquor Store, the other Arab store, where you played illegal numbers hoping you hit the 'hood jackpot.

Those were the hangout spots, the parking lots at the stores on both sides of NW 22nd Avenue, before you cross the tracks.

At any given time, especially on the weekend, you were going to see ten or more people sipping something, smoking something and vibing.

It wasn't too packed, but you would see old coons that dressed good, and young, dope niggahs with fly chicks. Bobby Liquor Store was shut down, but eventually it was opened back up under new management.

My childhood friend, TT's dad, owned a Car Wash at the gates just before you crossed the tracks. His name was Black Pete. He used to be with Rick Brownie, another big time dope dealer. I respected him.

We called him the Mayor of Opa-Locka because he did more for the community of Opa-Locka than the mayor and politicians themselves.

He bought the neighborhood kids clothes, shoes, paid medical bills, helped the people pay bills, provided food.

I wasn't justifying how he made his money, but he took care of the community as well.

He had the respect of the streets, ten-toes down.

My church raised enough money to buy a two-story building further down NW 22nd Avenue, and NW 170th, in the cut, Carol City.

CHAPTER SIX:
FAMILY

My great-grandma was a foster parent. That was her source of income and how she got paid.

Pa-Pa fought in World War II. He also worked on the railroads.

Hard, manual labor in the blazing sun. On top of that, sometimes he was dying of thirst. When my great granddaddy left the railroad and the Army, he worked for Eastern Airlines until he retired, working on airplanes.

My great granddaddy worked all the time.

I wasn't saying that my great-grandmother was bougie, but before we came along, she had fur coats, sterling silverware with her initials on it, nice, beautiful, expensive furniture. After me and my siblings came, it was like we all broke everything down.

Or at least that's the way it seemed…

I never understood when she said, "I gave up everything for y'all."

When it came to my mother, my great-grandparents at the time weren't the type that would comfort me or anything like that when I went through any type of emotional abuse.

Granted, my great-grandparents would try to intervene when my mom was acting a fool or said harsh things to me.

They would try to keep her locked out the door, but I never felt a part of their family. I always felt like an outsider looking in. I always felt like I didn't belong, that the family I was given was somehow a mistake because I was going through so much emotional abuse.

To calm myself, I fell in love with music. Music always determined my feelings. If I listened to happy music, I was happy. If I listened to rap, I was thinking about who I wanted to fuck up or what I was going to do. If I listened to 2 Live Crew, I was pop, pop, pop and twerking.

I felt hopeless when dad was sent to the big house. My big brother, Vare, followed my mom's lead by beating on me, too. I used to always have black eyes.

My dad told me not to worry because when he got out of prison, he was going to stop them from abusing me.

I used to be scared. I couldn't fight all that good. Once my big brother taught me how to fight it was going down.

He used to make me fight the boys in school like I was a whole nigga. I didn't back down from nobody, nor did I run from anybody.

I remember when I was in the 4th grade, and he was in the 5th grade.

There was this cute boy with good hair named Christian that was new to Nathan B. Young Elementary School. If my life ever becomes a book and I wrote about it, my classmates will know exactly who I was talking about.

Christian was horrible. He came to class and acted like he ran things. The new kid on the block tried to run the block . He had a bad attitude. I didn't like his ass.

Honestly, it didn't bother me. But it obviously bothered my big brother. Apparently, Christian got slick at the mouth with my big brother during recess.

I was clueless that my big brother and Christian had any issues. All I know was that, since my brother was a grade level above me, a bunch of kids ran up to me and said, "Oh, oh....you and Christian are about to fight after school!"

I was confused. "Huh? What are y'all talking about?" I asked.

My big brother set me up to fight Christian after school. I was the last to know. I didn't think I'd be a contender in a fight I had no knowledge of. I wasn't scared to fight, so it was what it was. Now everybody wanted to see us fight.

Later on, I saw my big brother. I approached him. "Hey Vare, what's this I'm hearing about me fighting after school?"

He said, "That lil nigga Christian talking shit. He's too young for me to fight. Y'all are in the same grade. He's more your speed. I'm gonna make you kick his ass."

I couldn't turn back now.

After school, in the back by the P.E. court, you could see the iron double doors by the kindergarten classes. There was also a gate we could exit from as well.

A lot of kids were ready to see a fight. There was already a huge circle formed. The noise level was deafening. Everybody was rowdy and instigating.

As I walked up the hall towards the back, there were two ends. Doors to the left end and the right end.

I exited the doors to the right and Christian was standing in the middle of a sea of people, in the circle. I was ready. My brother taught me how to box, how to hold my set up (fists), how to swing, punch and maneuver. How to breathe and all. Just because I was a girl didn't mean shit.

"Just keep your head up baby girl," Vare said.

I put my guard up, Christian did the same.

My big brother taught me to aim at the face and go for broke. I gave him a two piece knuckle sandwich. Bap, bap!

He stumbled backward amidst a sea of praise, baby. It was lights out, game over. Got his ass kicked by a female.

I knocked some of his teeth loose. He was bleeding from the mouth.

The kids stirred up even more drama with the side remarks. I got my props that day.

I walked off and went about my business.

I bet Christian humbled himself after that. I bet he didn't try to run the class like he was our leader again.

I bet he didn't talk shit to my big brother anymore. What my brother didn't realize was that when he taught me how to fight, when he taught me how to breathe, how to maneuver, how to punch, how to bob and weave, how to fight men, it backfired because of one of his friends.

I didn't want to say his name because everybody knew him, not that I gave a shit. He was one of my brother's raggedy-mouth friends that was named after his big money father. All of his top teeth were, chile, I better not.

My brother and Yuck Mouth was the same age. They used to always rank on each other.

What I meant by "ranking" was that they cracked jokes on each other every time they were in each other's company.

I grew tired of Yuck Mouth talking shit to me. I wasn't my brother, nor did I find him funny.

I should two-piece-special his ass! I wanted to fight Yuck Mouth because he kept trying to crack jokes on me. Whether I was coming home from school or coming up the block, I was the butt of jokes when he saw me with my brother.

My brother found it funny, except for me.

Alright, muthafuckah, since he taught me how to fight dude, then I was going to fight his friend.

We could rumble. It was now or never. I ran up on his raggedy mouth ass, and the funniest thing happened.

My brother picked me up and slammed me in the bushes. It took me by complete surprise.

Whereas he set up the fight between Christian and I, and stayed in the background when we fought, he picked me up and threw me in the bushes over a yuck mouth nigga? You fuck ass bitch!

"I'm gonna catch you by yourself and beat your ass, bitch!" I yelled at Yuck Mouth.

CHAPTER SEVEN
UNWANTED

I went home mad as fuck. I was so upset I told my great-grandma that he picked me up and threw me in the damn cherry bush on the corner of her house by Segal Park.

That shit hurt, and I wasn't talking about my pride and ego. Those stiff, thin branches didn't feel good.

It was a well-trimmed bush, so those sharp ass sticks poked me in the back and on my legs.

The cherry bush belonged to my friend Edward Johnson, God rest his soul.

He was sixteen years young when he committed suicide, breaking my heart and the hearts of the community at large.

I thought about my brother slamming me in the bushes over Yuck Mouth raggedy-baby-teeth ass for days to come.

My brother never got in trouble for slamming me. He always got away with murder. He never experienced a beating in his natural life, no matter what he did.

He was already beating on me, and that intensified even more because he was getting away with it.

I never understood why my brother was abusing me.

I was walking on my confidence and self-esteem every time he punched on me. A lot of the black eyes I had were the result of my brother's fists. He took joy in bullying me.

He wouldn't even fight Christian in school. He claimed because Christian was younger than him, that he was around my age group, was the reason why I should fight him.

But he turned around and beat on me.

He looked at me with disgust. He called me dirty, and all kinds of stuff. Maybe that was why he slammed me in the bushes. Because he agreed with everything Yuck Mouth was saying, which would explain why he laughed with the intensity that he did.

I did not know what his problem was with me.

The sad part about it all was that he taught me how to fight, ride a bike, and pop a bubble with bubble gum.

He did teach me those three things.

Outside of that, I felt that his life's purpose was to make me miserable, torture me, punch on me, talk down to me, and make me feel lesser than.

Like I didn't deserve to live. I felt low and unloved when it came to him.

I wallowed in the pain and betrayal my brother continuously inflicted on me.

My whole life he treated me harshly.

From the time I moved into my great-grandma Patsy's house when my daddy was in prison until now, he always saw the worst in me. Out in the streets, I started smoking weed.

It helped me to escape what I was going through and what I had to deal with.

I never liked marijuana, no type of drugs or alcohol ever in my life, because of my mom's history with drugs.

Nonetheless, once I ran away from home and ventured outside of Opa-Locka, things changed.

I wasn't going to lie, a lot of people claimed they were not followers, but it was bullshit.

When you were forced to survive you did what you had to do.

Ninety-eight percent of the shit I got into was the result of watching someone else, or being influenced by older women in my family that was giving me "guidance," but no directions.

Don't believe the hype when people tell you they never followed anyone.

Ask yourself, what made you smoke a joint when you first did, or what made you have sex when you first had it.

There was always someone influencing me until I started figuring things out on my own.

When I was ten years old, I met two girls that I grew up with. One lived around the corner from my house. She was fifteen, and the other girl was fourteen.

I was hanging with them.

To my recollection they were running away from home, so I started running away from home. I ran away from home because I got tired of the pain. I was tired of my mother abusing me.

I was tired of my brother abusing me.

I wanted to run away from all the chaos and leave the catastrophe behind and just go somewhere peaceful, a place where I felt the abuse would stop.

I was tired of being abused. Let me be clear. I thought my whole world was Opa-Locka.

It's only four miles long and wide. I never knew a bigger world existed outside of my neighborhood.

When I ran away, I found out, to my surprise. Mind you, I was born on 143rd street and 22nd Place across from Segal's Park, by Ali Baba. Anybody that was from there knew about the Triangle. It was called the Triangle because of all the murders and robberies that transpired during the early 80s that had become urban legend.

The area was inevitably barricaded off by the county. There was only one way in and one way out.

Despite the high crime, no matter who got killed, robbed, gagged, didn't matter, we still partied on the corner and had a good time.

Then Big Daddy Conch was killed, along with an innocent bystander, a young dude named Romeo or Ramio, something like that, on Ali Baba.

Big Daddy Conch had a bar on 21 Jump Street.

The young dude was one of my friend's cousins. He was going to college, had everything going for himself.

I remember a time Mike Tyson drove through Opa-Locka. I was a little girl, so I couldn't run to Ali Baba to get a glimpse of him.

A lot of celebrities have come through Opa-Locka, but the local crime quickly overshadowed it.

There were so many murders. Also, family members killed family members.

There were a lot of unsolved murders.

With all the murders, the average person knew who killed who, but the code of the streets kept invisible muzzles on their lips.

Nobody said a word.

Remember, I was born on 143rd and 22nd Place.

Before that, you have 22nd Avenue, and four or five additional blocks before Nathan B. Young Elementary School.

I could name several of my friends that were murdered on each of those streets.

CHAPTER EIGHT
BABY DADDY

I met Fat Boi Hicks on Segal Park. I was ten years old, and he was twelve. There was a lot of people on the Park that day. I stood out. That was what attracted Fat Boi to me. He wore suede Bally shoes and the outfit to match. He brandished a whole bunch of jewelry, and he had long hair.

My natural hair was long as well, to my elbows. We were actually childhood friends. His daddy's name was Isaac Hicks. Big Ike, he was a big drug dealer from the early '80s.

I used to always see him visit because his grandma stayed around the corner from my great-grandma in Opa-locka.

His mama grew up with my mama and my daddy knew his daddy and all of them used to hang out at the big house in the 'hood.

I knew their family too, but I really didn't know him because he was hardly around.

He asked for my phone number, then he inquired about who I was. I told him who I was, and all the while, he was best friends with my big brother Vare.

When Vare wasn't coming home, he stayed the night with Fat Boi at his daddy Big Ike's house. Vare started selling drugs when he was ten years old.

He was already out there, moving and shaking, so when me and Fat Boi met, they were around the same age.

Fat Boi was my first boyfriend.

At that time, I was gullible. He was trying to have sex with me. I was scared because I was a virgin. We kissed, but I would never let him touch me on my intimate areas.

In the beginning, we talked a lot whenever he visited on the weekends, and on holidays. We got to know each other.

I listened to him tell me about his lifestyle and the luxury of being a big dope dealer's son. He used to tell me stories about how he used to fuck prostitutes at their house.

Mind you, he was only twelve.

He used to tell me how he used to see pounds of cocaine and loads of money.

Inevitably, his mom and Big Ike was raided by the Feds and they were sent to prison. Fat Boi moved in with his grandma permanently, and he was best friends with my big brother. We became even closer.

We eventually started having sex. I was twelve years old when I did it for the first time. I was in love with Fat Boi. He was my world.

I was so bold, I walked into my great grandma's house, looked my Mama in the face and said, "Charlotte! I need birth control."

She frowned at me. "You little bitch! What do you need birth control for?"

"Because I'm having sex!"

"You're having sex? I ain't killing no baby, bitch and you're not getting on no birth control."

"I guess I'll be having a baby and I ain't using no condoms!"

And I walked off.

At this point I had already started running away from home, I started fighting in the streets, and I was ready to get with her ass if she tried me. I was ready to fight her at that moment.

I had already said in my mind, *If my motherfucking Mama touch me again, I'm gonna fuck her up! I'm tired of her!*

I was tired of her. I never hit my Mama back, not one time during all those years of abuse.

From six years old until the age of twelve, this lady abused me.

And I never hit her back.

I never hit her back!

Fat Boi had a lot of money for his age. We'd take the bus to the movies and do things together.

The only life he knew was peddling drugs.

Now that his parents were in the Big House, he stepped up and started selling drugs as a teenager.

His big brother, Headquarters, was in a gang, heavy.

Fat Boi was the first boy I ever kissed. He was already spoiled with cars and shit. Being that we were young, that environment caused me to grow up fast.

And that came with consequences.

CHAPTER NINE: RAPE

Fat Boi didn't know, but one of his friends raped me. Being that he was a young boy, he started bragging about us being together, and that we were sexually active. That probably made me look more appealing to his young friends, giving them the wrong type of thoughts.

I didn't want to say anything about the sexual assault. I was too embarrassed and ashamed because the older boy that raped me was his friend. I felt like I was slightly to blame, and I was going to explain why.

My great-grandma had just bought me some flat boots that came up to my knees. Also, I had on a little cute dress that dropped a little above my knees.

I felt like I was pretty that day. It was the late afternoon. Bright outside. I had **fell** in love with Fat Boi. I started walking down the street from my great-grandma's house. I was singing and dancing to myself. I was on the corner. I felt pretty. Just feeling myself.

Psst...Psst...Psst.

I looked back. I saw one of Fat Boi's older friends, named Raymond. They were the same age. He was red skinned. I'd never forget his name. He was a handsome young boy, but I didn't like him like that.

Psst....

"What do you want? What do you want?" I said fast.

"Come here," he whispered. "Come here..."

"For what? *For what?* What do you want? Come here for what?"

I didn't take it as him being sneaky when he was saying, "Just come here, come here really quick, come here really quick."

"What do you want, Raymond?"

"Come here..."

Reluctantly, I strolled down the sidewalk. The position of the house where I was, and my great-grandma's house down the street, you couldn't see far back, so no one could see him from the front of the house. He was on the side of the house.

When I walked up to him, he brutally grabbed me by the neck and started dragging me. Where my great-grandma's house was, there was a house next to it, there was a street, and a church house as well.

There was an abandoned school bus in that yard.

"What are you doing?" I asked him, scared. *"What are you doing?"*

He was fifteen-years old. I was twelve. "You're going with me!" he demanded.

"Why, what are you doing?"

"Shut up! Shut up! Shut up!"

He pushed me through the school bus doors. I could vaguely remember the latch on the school bus window was broken. I didn't remember the doors being wide open.

Raymond slammed me down on the school bus bench and we were tussling, and wrestling.

I was crying and begging him, "Please, don't do this! *Don't do this!"*

"Be quiet! Be Quiet!"

I already had on a short dress with no shorts on underneath. Maybe I was being grown, because my auntie let wear a pair of panties that tied on either side.

That made it easy access for him. And he raped me. He didn't hit me, but he pinned me down and did what he did to me on that abandoned school bus.

It was so quick, it was so fucking quick, it was so fucking quick. He came inside of me. After it was over, he stayed on the bus, and I ran home.

I couldn't remember what I did when I got home. I saw him again a day later. He was sitting on the porch with my big brother, my baby daddy, and a couple other dudes, at Fat Boi's house.

I was walking up the block. Raymond gave me a terrified look because he thought I was going to say something, but little did he know that I was too afraid to say anything.

He didn't try to make up a lie, or anything. He didn't say anything. And I didn't. I felt guilty because I was on the corner prancing. So, in a way I felt like I probably asked for it.

I didn't go up to the porch with them. I kept walking. Fat Boi had a screened-in porch with bars. I didn't see Raymond anymore after that. I knew that he went to prison.

I didn't know at what age. I didn't know what happened to him. But I did hear rumors about how he was raping his sister in those apartments.

I never told anybody what he did to me. I didn't know how true the rumor was, but the niggas knew he was doing that to his own sister.

I started having sex when I was twelve. I lost my virginity to my baby daddy. I was raped shortly after on the abandoned school bus, and raped a second time after that, and I was still twelve.

I was on NW 22nd Avenue, and 143rd, looking for an older woman that I befriended. My great-grandma's house was there, my baby daddy's house was in front of me on the block, and the next block was NW 22nd Avenue where the apartments were located.

I knew a lot of people in the apartments. I went up there and I asked my older friend's older brother where she was.

He said, "She's not here."

There was another older man there, and he was my older cousin's age. I was twelve, they had to be about nineteen.

He was like, "What's up."

"Nothing, I got a boyfriend."

"So what? What's up with you?"

"Nothing."

"That's my sister's friend," said her brother.

"I don't care," said the dude. "You're acting like its all of that."

The next thing I knew, he had grabbed me, threw me in the truck, and the girl's brother drove off. They were taking me towards Liberty City.

I was terrified. I kept begging him to turn back around.

"Please, what are you doing? Please turn back around," I begged them.

The dude on the passenger side kept elbowing me in the side and telling me to shut up. I kept begging my friend's brother to take me back. They took me to Large Mount Projects.

When they pulled up, the boy snatched me out of the truck by my hair and he kept punching me in my ribs. I was too scared to fight back. I was terrified.

We went through the back door of the house and his Mama was in the kitchen.

"If you say something I'm going to kill you," he threatened.

His Mama asked, "Are y'all alright, are y'all alright?"

"Yea, Ma, we're alright," he said and kept it moving.

He took me into his room, slammed me on the bed, and I kept begging, "Please, please, don't rape me! Please, don't rape me!"

I was so scared. When I looked at his penis it was big and red, like it was infected.

I kept begging, "Please, please, please don't rape me..."

"I'm gonna put a condom on, I'm gonna put a condom on."

He put a condom on. I looked up and there were a lot of men at the window, watching. He kept punching me in my side and put a pillow over my face while I was screaming. He bit me on my titty.

And he raped me.

I ran out of his house when he finished. I jumped back in the truck with my friend's brother, hollering and crying about what happened.

"Don't call the police," he pleaded, "because he will go to jail. I didn't know the dude was going to do that to you. Please, please don't call the police."

He drove me back to apartments in Opa-Locka. I ran all the way home. I took a shower. My great-grandma kept asking me what's wrong, what's wrong.

I just sat in the tub and scrubbed myself, scrubbed myself, and scrubbed myself over and over.

CHAPTER TEN:
STOLEN CAR

I remember the first stolen car I got in; well, actually the car wasn't stolen. I was still twelve years old, so was my cousin Wanna. My cousin Yaya and Goo-Goo was fourteen.

Let me tell it, we were too fast in the ass. We met these grown ass men. Of course, we lied about our ages. We made like we were older teenagers, like eighteen and nineteen. The men were in their early twenties.

I didn't remember who exchanged numbers with the men, but we wound up calling them. We spoke to the dudes on the phone, and they came to scoop us up in two different cars.

One was an old looking stuffer car, and the other vehicle was fixed up all nice and shit with rims and music. The leather seats matched the color scheme of the outside.

We thought we were the shit! You couldn't tell us we weren't doing it. We looked good in our hoochie shit (bathing suits), since the dudes said they were taking us to the beach.

It was four of us and four of them. Once we arrived at Haulover Beach, the four dudes ventured off far into the salt water, in areas that were not safe for anyone. They were trying to convince us to follow suit.

Me and Wanna was close. We liked the same things. Yaya wasn't fast like us, but she liked the boys. Me and Wanna's grown ass was about to go in the water them, but Yaya and GooGoo stayed on the hot ass sand.

Mind you, the fellas left their pants, shirts and belongings on the sand.

.   We looked back at Wanna and Goo-Goo. We wondered why they didn't come with us. Yaya was going through the pants and shorts pockets, being nosey as hell. Yaya started dangling a set of car keys at us. Wanna and I looked at each other, baffled.

Why was she dangling the dude's car keys?

I grinned. "Wanna, I think Yaya is going to steal the dude's car."

Wanna was laughing. "Shit, why not."

"Come on!" Yaya yelled out to us.

.   I shook my head. "Yea, her crazy ass is about to steal their car!"

Once we got out of the water, Wanna and I rushed up to our girls.

"Shit, leggo!"

We played follow the leader.

We wasted no time taking the dude's car. We went joy riding. I hopped in the passenger seat of the hooptie, the old-looking ass car.

Yaya volunteered to drive. Wanna and GooGoo hopped on the back seat.

Wait, we weren't at no muthafucking Haulover. We were at South Beach. I'd never been to South Beach before, so I had no clue.

Even though we had their keys, there was one major problem. Neither one of us knew how to drive a vehicle, and that didn't stop us either.

Yaya backed that shit up and drove the car up the street amidst our celebratory cheers. She was whipping it, until the bitch hit and ran over a parking meter. It came out of the pavement with a piece of the sidewalk still on the foundation.

"Bitch, are you blind?"

"You didn't see that fucking meter?"

Everybody panicked. I yelled out loud. "Y'all calm down, shit! A bitch is trying to think. Okay…" I had a plan. "Get yawl asses out! Now!"

I followed my first mind, my gut instinct.

"I'll drive! Hurry! Hurry! Get out and y'all push the car back as I put it in reverse."

The Lord, God, Jehovah, Jesus or whoever one prayed to must have been with us that day because they listened to me and did what I said.

Once I successfully backed up off the meter, they got inside, and I drove. It was my first time driving. Yup, it was. I hadn't even stolen my daddy car yet, but that was another story.

I was excited, nervous, all that. There was so much water and tall ass bridges on either side of the highway, but I wasn't scared or discouraged.

My squad was frightened. They panicked.

I snapped. "Yawl shut the fuck up and calm down. I can't focus on the road. We good right nah."

"Bitch you're gonna kill us!" Yaya prophesied, even though it wasn't going to happen.

"Dam, gurl be quiet! I need to focus!"

I had common sense. I'd seen enough grown people drive, so I knew to stay between the white lines, signal, change lanes and check mirrors; the pedal was to *go*, and the brake was to *stop*.

Once we got to our 'Hood in Opa Locka, we were zooming up the block.

Chapter Eleven:
Trouble

We stopped by my house. To my surprise one of my siblings rushed up to me like she was about to pass out. "Oooh, gurl!"

"Oh, gurl, what?"

It looked like she saw a ghost. "What did y'all do? Y'all stole dem bois' car and they're looking for y'all with guns! They were here at our house!"

We were confused. "They have all guns blazing over an unappealing ass car?" I asked, lost.

Something didn't add up, but I knew we fucked up!

We were scared out of our mind. "Why are they looking for us with guns? It can't be just about a car with no value...."

Furthermore, the armed dope bois had been to Tiny and Wanna's house looking for us.

GooGoo's cousin asked, "Goob, what the fuck have you've gotten yourself into? Those crazy niggas came to all of our homes with enough guns to start a dam war."

You couldn't imagine how paranoid we were.

I had no idea how they knew where we lived, especially since they initially picked us up on the way to the beach on 22nd Avenue.

Oh, shit. I knew how. The snitching ass bitches around the 'Hood told them when they inquired about us. If I wasn't mistaken Keyell Hollis told them. He was like a cousin.

Don't get me wrong, I loved him, but damn. What if they were human traffickers? What if they killed us on the spot? He would have led them right to us with no shame.

Despite it, we were still joyriding in a car that was wrecked in the front, speeding up the very streets we were being hunted.

Out of the blue the armed bois spotted us.

Oh, shit! I mashed down on the gas pedal and hauled ass down NW 22nd Avenue, headed towards Liberty City. I was only twelve years old. With no destination in sight, we were on a real mission with no way out.

We were on a high-speed chase. I ran stop signs and red lights. I didn't give a fuck. I mashed the pedal to the metal.

God had to have still been with us. Looking over her shoulder from the back seat, Yaya shouted, "Turn into Scott's projects! *Turn into Scott's projects!* I know some dudes up in there!"

One of the dude's names was Peanut.

I took her advice.

At breakneck speed I turned into the projects too fast, and I lost control of the vehicle. Boom! I wrecked the car, putting us in a dangerous situation.

It must have been the adrenaline because we all hopped out and took off running for our lives. We hauled ass like we chased Olympic gold in track and field.

Yaya led us to Peanut's crib. Banging on the door in desperation, he let us in, locking the door. Police squad cars pulled up on the scene to investigate the crash.

They uncovered keys upon keys of pure cocaine from the trunk. Word traveled fast in the projects, especially with the authorities present.

"There was loads of cocaine in the trunk, ya'll," I said in disbelief. They couldn't believe it either.

What if we were caught and pulled over by the cops and they discovered that we were not only underage, but cocaine was in the trunk that we were unaware of.

You thought the police was going to believe the drugs didn't belong to us, let alone a small army of angry niggas that was already hunting us down?

Now I saw why the dope bois were after us whether if it ended in life or death. Now it made sense.

The drug bois kept the drugs in the trunk a secret when they were asking people around Opa-Locka about us and our whereabouts. They put out the word that they were going to kill us.

Now we were too scared to go home. I felt like a fugitive at twelve. We were extremely paranoid. I wasn't even into drugs yet. I only experimented with drinking.

For days we didn't go home. We were scared as fuck. The dope bois were still looking for us. I felt like they weren't leaving until we were found.

And if they found us, we die.

You know what saved us? They found out our ages, that we were minors, barely teenagers.

When word traveled around about our ages, the dope bois changed their tune.

"What? A bunch of kids jacked our shit? Ah, nawl! They lied to us about their ages...."

Yes. Lying about our ages wound up being our saving grace.

We still didn't go home. We were getting on the bus across the track by Ali Baba. When we walked across the tracks through the little cut my Mama saw us.

She was pissed. Smoke came out of her ears.

"GET YO MUTHAFUCKIN' ASS HOME, BITCH!"

Oh, shit!

Yaya and Wanna's parents had been searching relentlessly for them as well.

She glared at my crew. She made them go home and she meant business.

One thing about our parents back in that era, they beat our asses in Opa Locka. They believed in discipline, even though I got away with everything when it came to my great granddaddy.

If one of our parents saw the other parent's child, we better listen to that concerned parent because the village it took to raise a child was able to spank our asses. They didn't give a fuck how you felt about it.

And at home we got our asses beaten again. We were spanked in school and all. Everywhere we went we got our asses whipped. Maybe if it remained that way the crime rate wouldn't be so high, or kids wouldn't be institutionalized, or they wouldn't be strung out on drugs.

Just maybe.

A child had to stay in a child's place and stay outta grown-up conversations.

I hoped the good, the bad, the ugly and the crazy of this experience could help someone else make better choices with their lives by the mistakes and bad decisions I made with my own.

That was my first experience in a stolen car that someone else stole. I was just the driver that took over when things turned sour. I guessed I was an accessory.

I didn't take those keys out of the dope boi's pants. I wasn't bold enough to steal nobody's car at that age.

That's what happened on our journey. Being homeless for two days. We lived from pillow to pole. Eating chips, and drinking water the best way that we could.

We were hungry, starving. Our stomachs were touching our backs. We were too scared to go home, but when my Mama caught me, the whole ordeal was officially over.

We never saw the boys again, thank God.

Truth be told, I didn't know if the niggas got the dope out of the trunk of the crashed car before the cops arrived or not.

My girl's decision to steal a car almost got us murdered.

Chapter Twelve:
The Hurt

As time went by, I found out I was pregnant about two months before my thirteenth birthday. Fat Boi was happy about our baby. I was at his brother Headquarters' house when he had stripper women walking around naked. I was sitting on the couch, pregnant.

His two little sisters were also sitting there. They were younger than me. We watched hos prance around with their titties and pussies out, with no shame.

Fat Boi would go in the room with his brother and the naked bitches. I didn't think anything of it. I didn't say anything because I was naïve.

Fat Boi then started beating the fuck out of me. He would watch his big brother beat his girlfriends, so he started beating on me.

I attended a school called "Cope," a school for pregnant teenagers that wanted to continue their education.

Me, along with a few girls, were the first attendees of the school when it first opened. It was a new place that helped teenage mothers.

My stomach was flat all the way up to the eighth month of my pregnancy. My friends kept saying, "You're not pregnant! You're not pregnant!"

"But I am pregnant!" I responded.

"If you are, then how many months along are you?"

"Five!" I spoke.

"How many months are you?"

"Six!" I answered.

"How many months along are you?"

"Seven!" I responded.

I was going to the doctor on a regular basis, but my friends were in disbelief. "But where is your baby bump?" they asked.

My stomach was up and down like a flat washboard. I could understand why people didn't believe I was pregnant, but I was.

After eight months, I woke up and couldn't see my damn feet. Just like that, I had a big baby bump.

I didn't know if anybody could relate to that type of pregnancy, having a flat stomach from the beginning to eight months.

I could wear a halter top and daisy dukes. My stomach was flat. At eight months my stomach went bloop! It was sitting in my lap. I was wobbling.

That didn't stop me. I didn't know any better.
I was still wearing daisy dukes

My baby daddy would take me to his house,
cut my clothes off of me, then sent me home. I still
put something else on.

Shortly after, I was sitting at the kitchen table.
I was big...and swollen. My great grandma's God
daughter, Janie, handed my great grandma Patsy
her Sunday dinner plate.

There were stories about Janie, good and bad,
in our family. That was another story.

She always cooked Sunday dinner for my great
grandma. Every Sunday she cooked for her and
fixed her Sunday plate.

There was a centerpiece on the table that held
my great-grandma's scissors, pecans, and
miscellaneous stuff she called "what nots."

Great-grandma always shared her food with us.
Pa-Pa didn't like that. He always bought her a
Whopper from Burger King because she loved
them. It was big as hell. You could barely hold the
burger with two hands.

When I say "grandma," I meant my great-
Grandma Patsy. We used to get corrected all the
time. She wasn't my "grandma," she was my
Mama's grandma, and my Granny (great-grandma).

Great-grandma Patsy used to cut the Whopper
into little pieces, and she shared it with every last
one of us. Mind you, there was fourteen of us
living together in one house. Pa-Pa fussed about it,
but he always bought my great grandma that big ass
Whopper when it was all said and done.

"I'm still not gonna bring it," he'd say. "That's something special I do for Mama!"

He referred to my great-grandma as "Mama."

My great-grandma shared her Sunday dinner plate with me.

I was at the table with her when Mama entered the room, gripping a silver can of Schlitz malt liquor beer with the blue bull on the front. Yup, she acted just like that bull. A bully. She was high as hell. You could see it all in her face.

Her eyes were red, and her mouth twisted into a frown. Her light skin was sunburned. Her complexion was red and jolly, like Santa Claus.

She was looking for blood. Her shark-looking face reminded me of one that was about to attack.

I already said in my mind that I was ready for her. I knew how to fight, I wasn't scared of her anymore, and I never hit her back, but today was a new day.

I was eight months pregnant with a baby. If that lady hit me again, I was gonna fuck her up. I was tired of being her punching bag when she couldn't get high, or because I was ugly, or because of my darker skin color.

She beat me because she didn't like how I talked, she hated that I favored my Daddy's side of the family, and she abused me because of my long hair. Whatever. There was always something.

"Grandma, I need some money!" Mama said.

"I don't have nothing for you," great-grandma responded flatly.

"You don't have nothing for me?" Mama repeated in disbelief.

"That's what I said!"

Mama walked up to us and knocked the centerpiece off the table, and it hit the floor.

She was cussing and fussing. Me and my great grandma was still eating, sharing a plate. I kind of chuckled.

She glared at me. "Bitch, what's funny? I'll fuck you up!"

"You're bad!" I retorted. "Do it, Superwoman!"

She wound her hand back and she slapped the dog shit out of me. Guess what? I was still sitting in the chair by my great-grandma.

I hopped my pregnant ass up with balled-up fists, put up my guard and two-pieced that ho right between those red eyes: Bap. Bap!

I could fight like a boxer. Hitting her between the eyes stunned her ass. I gave her two black eyes. In an instant, I grabbed a knife off the table, it was like a saw knife, and chopped that ho. One of the blades was stuck right between her forehead and her hairline.

My great-grandma called the police then, ha! She called the police then!

I glared at Mama, and I wasn't playing with her ass. "Ho, if you ever in your *motherfucking life* put your hands on me again," I said, "I'm gonna bury your crack head smoking ass, bitch! *Those days are over with!* Put your hands on me one more time, bitch, I'm gonna kill you!"

Shortly after, the police arrived at the house. I was a pregnant thirteen year old. Mama slapped the fuck out of a pregnant teenager, a minor. And I had already two-pieced that ho, giving her two black eyes. Blood was coming from her head.

The Opa-Locka police said, "This is how we're gonna do it. Nobody's going to jail because if anybody is going to jail, both of you are going to jail! Since you (Charlotte) jumped on a pregnant teenager, and you (Lashonta) used a knife, we're going call it even and let this go."

I rode with Pa-Pa to Robin Hood by Arcola Lakes Park, by my grandma's residence (my Mama's Mama), so I could cool off. Meanwhile, he was telling her what happened between me and her daughter.

I heard my grandma say that Charlotte knew better than to be jumping on me. She knew better, and now wasn't the time to be abusing me while I was pregnant, so whatever happened, happened.

I was shocked that she said that because she never showed concern or said anything in my defense before. She never showed me or my daddy's kids any type of affection. That was the first time I ever defended myself, and the first time I ever hit my Mama back.

You know what? Mama never put her hands on me again. The bitch didn't touch me anymore. I was scared to go there with my grandma because I did use a knife on her daughter, my Mama.

I promised on my unborn baby I was going to kill Mama if she touched me again. I promised you!

She beat on me for too long, for nothing! She beat me for years, for nothing! She damaged me. And now she wanted to abuse me while I was pregnant.

Oh, no, bitch! I wasn't about to have her beating on me while I was carrying my child.

Mind you, my big brother Vare picked up that abusive shit from my Mama, too. When he didn't get his way, he knocked shit off tables, punched holes in the TVs, and other shit. Mama had no idea that her actions rubbed off on her kids.

My baby sister Gin once tried to bully my baby cousin, Qweeta, my auntie's daughter. Gin was jumping on Qweeta, fighting her.

"Oh no! Oh no, Gin!" I said, "You're not about to start that! You're not gonna do that! You're not about to start doing Mama's bullying in this house!"

I taught my baby cousin Qweeta how to fight. Once she learned, I told Gin, "Since you want to fight, go ahead and fight! Because Qweeta know how to fight now!"

I let them go outside in the dirt and Qweeta wore Gin's ass out! Bap, bap, bap, bap, bap! Whooped her ass!

"Now you know, if you want to jump on Qweeta, she's gonna give you a run for your money."

Problem solved.

Anyway, Mama never touched me anymore after that. I promise you to God, since that incident, when I fucked that bitch up, she didn't put her hands on me again.

Guess what? That was when my fighting days started. I was already in the streets. I was like, okay, I wasn't dealing with no one's shit anymore.

I was already thirteen and pregnant, the year before I was raped twice, I was too scared to fight back, and I wasn't the fighting type of person.

I was bullied and abused by my own Mama, no one did a thing to stop it, and now I was pregnant at thirteen? And I was not scared to fight back.

Oh, it was on and cracking. It was going down after that. Only if I had that strength a year before, when I was raped twice.

Only if I had that strength and courage. I would have been able to protect myself, but I was scared. I didn't like to fight. I wanted peace, love, and happiness.

Unfortunately, I had to get out of that mentality.

CHAPTER THIRTEEN: PREGNANCY

My auntie Aretha and my Pa-Pa were the ones taking me to my doctor appointments. They registered me at the school for pregnant girls, COPE. I remember when I was at COPE. They allowed a pregnant mother's baby daddy to attend the school if she wanted him to, but he would have to sign in. He would have to go to school Monday through Friday, and do schoolwork as well. He could participate with her in classes because it was a special school.

We were given snacks throughout the school day. They had a daycare in the school for the kids. We were taught about the inside and outside of our bodies, our organs, and the extremities.

I loved whoever came up with the COPE school. That was the best idea ever! They made school fun! I loved the activities. During one of the activities, we had to draw the female's body and we had to name the organs on it. The breasts, and the vagina, we had to name it. On the male drawing we had to name the penis...we had to draw a line to each part with the right name of the body or the organ.

I found that to be very educational and fun at the same time. We were openly drawing pussies and dicks and we were learning about it.

I learned that the vagina lips had names. I thought it was funny. I thought education was funny. The lips on the outside was the labia majora, and the folds of skin on the inside that led to the vagina was the labia minora. And I was like, what?

And then the little man in the boat. I wondered what she was talking about.

"It's called a clitoris," my teacher said. I was repeating what I was being taught. It soaked in my brain like a sponge. So, that was a great idea to have a school for pregnant women.

They also showed us how to change the baby's diaper with baby dolls and how to fix the baby's bottle. I loved that.

Thinking about it, I was filled with joy. I was around other pregnant girls, and I was hearing their personal stories.

I found out that I wasn't the only one going through the things I'd been through. I wasn't alone. I felt normal, finally. I was around young pregnant girls that I could relate to, and they related to me.

There was one young girl who was about ten, maybe eleven years old. My right hand to God, it kind of fucked with my mind. She was white. Her baby's daddy, did you know how old he was? He was twenty-seven years old.

Our teacher asked us our baby daddy's names and he wrote the names on the chalk board. Once we were done, he left the names on display. He knew what he was doing.

He did the same exercise for the other classes, writing the girls' baby daddy's names on the chalkboard.

Because of it, there was one dude with five baby mamas at the school. He was stroking, chile. Word of mouth traveled around the whole school. That was The Talk! I was like, wow! I was glad nobody claimed my baby's daddy as their unborn child's father.

A girl name Priscilla saw my baby's daddy's name. She said something to a girl, and the pregnant girl told me, "Priscilla isn't pregnant from Fat Boi, but where Fat Boi's daddy was living, she was his girlfriend."

That was around the time before me, or after me, who knew. We were kids anyway.

I asked Fat Boi about Priscilla.

"Yea, I used to talk to her," he said, "before I met you. I didn't see her since my daddy got busted."

He saw her once, maybe twice after that in passing.

My white eleven year old pregnant friend's baby daddy was twenty-seven years old in the Army. And her parents were making her marry him. I thought she was fucking lying. That man came to COPE with a military outfit on.

Mind you, I had never asked the man was it true. He was probably her daddy or her uncle. That bitch said he was her baby's daddy.

I didn't think that was shocking because around that time, people didn't report grown men messing with young girls, especially in my neighborhood.

If they didn't report it in my 'hood, what made me think they reported it in hers? I felt that her situation was normal. That's why I believed her.

Then, I couldn't go into labor. My labor date was supposed to be in November. The doctor checked me and after examination they said everything was okay.

I thought the average pregnancy was supposed to be 9 months, three trimesters. You could be pregnant for up to 10 months or a little longer. I was pregnant 10 fucking months and still couldn't go into labor.

Medical personnel couldn't extend my labor deadline any longer because I was already pregnant for that long. I was a month past my due date. Because of it, I was admitted into the hospital. My baby wasn't coming out.

Then the doctor figured because I was so young, because I was 13 years old, maybe my pelvis wouldn't stretch. My baby wasn't supposed to be born in December; she was supposed to be born in November.

Now, during the second week in December, I was in the hospital. My auntie Aretha, as always, had my back. She was there for me. I love you, baby! I love you!

My auntie Aretha and my Pa-Pa had to admit me into the hospital. I had to stay in the hospital another two fucking weeks.

My blood pressure was sky high, and the doctor couldn't **induce my** labor if my blood pressure was too high.

My auntie Aretha comforted me. "Don't be scared now auntie baby," she said. I called my nieces and nephews auntie baby. If they didn't know where I got it from, they knew now.

When my auntie Aretha used to say "auntie baby" that used to make me feel so loved and comfortable with her. That's why I called my nieces and nephews "Auntie baby" because that's the love I have for them.

Auntie said, "You are going to hear a lot of women hollering, screaming, and crying. Especially the foreign women and the Haitian women with the aye-ya-ya-ya-ya-ah~" she did the chant. "~ don't get scared. It don't hurt that bad. You can cry, yes, it hurts, but acting foolishly, yelling, screaming, hollering, and disrespecting the doctors, don't do that. You hear me?"

I said, "Yes, auntie."

Once I was signed in, her and Pa-Pa left.

During my 2 weeks stay, the only person that came and saw me was my auntie and my Pa-Pa for the second time.

Surprisingly, my auntie snuck me a bag of banana chips. I loved banana chips. She put it in the drawer.

"Don't tell the nurse these chips are in here. Don't eat them all at one time. Eat them slow, okay?"

"Alright, auntie. I love you!"

I was so happy to have some banana chips because I was placed on a certain diet while I was in the hospital. There were certain things I couldn't eat, so the chips was a treat!

It was time to do my first ultrasound, to make sure the amniotic fluid in my sack wasn't low. It was low, but not dangerously low.

My baby was chilling like a villain in the motherfucker. When I was told I was having a girl I started crying with disappointment. Boo hoo.

"I want a boy...!"

CHAPTER FOURTEEN:
DELIVERY

Once my blood pressure was finally under control, it was Christmas Eve. The staff said, "Miss McCray we are about to induce your labor."

"Induce my labor?" I was confused. "What does that mean?"

The doctor explained to me that they were going to put something up my vagina, burst my water bag and then the labor started.

"Okay."

I wasn't slow at all about what I was going to go through delivering a baby because I learned through the COPE school beforehand, thank God, but I never heard about induced labor.

That was new to me. I thought my water bag would break normally, and I would start cramping. My cervix would dilate and when it dilated, my pelvic bone would start stretching and that was where the pain came from.

I was educated on all of that before I went into labor.

I wanted to clarify that I wasn't lost being there by myself. The doctor explained the procedure to me. I then saw him holding a yellow plastic rod.

Professionally, he stuck it up my private area and I felt all the liquid washing down my thighs. I was lying on a medical gurney, so I was alright.

"It's okay," the doctor said when it was over. "Now it's just a waiting game."

It was about 5 am, close to 6 o'clock, Christmas Eve. No problem. Come that afternoon, I was starting to feel pain down in my poo poo area.

The doctor said, "Okay, we're about to give you epidural."

Thank God for the COPE school again because they taught me what epidural was. They kept telling us, when it came to the shot, "Don't move! Don't move!"

They put emphasis on that. I learned the proper way to get it, and the consequences of moving with a needle in my spine. I was already mentally terrified. I couldn't move.

The nurse were saying, "Don't move. You can get paralyzed!"

They stuck the needle in, and I didn't jump. The pain went away, I was fine. It was late afternoon.

Well, it was between four and six p.m. The funny part about it was I suddenly started hearing the pregnant Haitian ladies cursing, hollering, and screaming aye-ye-ye-ye-yeh!

The reactions were just the way auntie described it. At this point it was going on 10 pm. The pain returned in my poo poo area, but it was a pushing sensation. It felt like I had to boo boo or push out something from my poo poo hole.

I was very polite. "Nurse. Nurse. Nurse. Nurse."

Nothing.

I shouted, "Nurse!"

The nurse came. "Yes, Miss McCray?"

"Ma'am I feel something down in my private and it feels like it's pushing, like a pressure down there."

"Okay, Miss McCray. You had an epidural shot. It's impossible for you to feel anything down there."

"Ma'am, I'm telling you what I feel!"

She walked away from me. Mind you, I did hear them gossiping about me, saying that I was thirteen and pregnant. I heard whispers along the hall during the two weeks I was there.

A few nurses even asked me about my parents, their whereabouts, or something of that nature.

"Nurse! I'm telling you something is pushing down there!"

She kept going. The bitch left.

Then, the pain worsened. I was rocking now, and I couldn't take it. Now I was holding my poo poo. I started screaming, *"Doc...tor! Please help me! Please help me! It hurts! It's something pushing!"*

The doctor came in. I remember this man's fingers. One of his fingers looked like the size of two of mine together.

That man was about stick those big ass shits up my poo poo? Yup, he put those three, fat sneaker fingers up my poo poo.

He shouted, "Get her prepared! The baby is in her vaginal canal!"

I told that lady I felt something pushing, I thought to myself, *and my baby was already in my vaginal canal, coming the fuck out.*

And that nurse ho kept walking away from me like I didn't know what I was talking about. I really feel like she treated me like that because I was a child.

"Do you want to wait until 12 midnight, Christmas Day to have your daughter?"

"Hell no!"

The staff rushed me to the delivery room. I learned the proper breathing techniques from the COPE school.

They told me to listen to the doctor. I did everything they told me to do. I pushed only when I was instructed to.

When they told me how to breathe, I did so. They asked me was someone there for me, and I answered no, I didn't have anyone there for me.

I was by myself.

My baby daddy would have come, but he couldn't because he was sick.

His aunt **Janis** told me that while I was in labor, he was throwing up, he was burning up and running a high fever. He was fucked up.

His auntie was helping him, and she verified that he couldn't make it off the couch. I found it funny. While I was in the hospital pushing out my baby, that motherfucker was on the couch, sick.

How ironic. Some people said that the baby daddy handled a woman in labor differently. I guessed he was feeling it in a whole new way.

I gave birth to Markeisha Janis Hicks on December 24th, 1991 at 10:21 p.m., Christmas Eve, my little gift. She was baked, she was healthy, and she was strong. And I love my "baldie!"

Well, her daddy called her baldie. I didn't call her that. She was my baby.

A bald head albino-like baby.

I used to pick on albino people. Lord, forgive me.

Please don't get offended with me, but I was a minor and I didn't know any better. I was just telling my truth.

I had nothing against albinos. Around that time, they were rare. You rarely saw one.

I wasn't educated on why the pigment of their skin gave them that appearance.

They weren't outcasts, but they were different.

We didn't know how to accept them.

Were they contagious?

We were kids.

We didn't know. But my baby was born pale as hell, with a bald head and stringy blonde strings atop her head.

And they glared.

Oh my God. I called my great-grandma crying and hollering. I had an albino baby and on top of that it was a girl.

My great-grandma Patsy said, "Calm down. Calm down."

My baby was so pretty, though, with her cute button nose and button lips. She was so cute, but she was bald head as hell.

You couldn't roll her hair with a piece of rice. She was bald, bald, bald. Baby oil slick bald. With strings of blonde hair.

I went to visit her at the nursery. I was looking at my baby through the picture window. And a white lady was already there.

"Hi," she said.

"Hi."

"Which one is your baby?"

I said, "Right there."

She was like, "Huh, right there, where the name says 'Hicks?'"

I said, "Yes."

"Is her dad white?"

I said, "Excuse me, but no. Her daddy is black."

"And you said that baby right there?"

"Yes."

"That baby is whiter than I am."

"I understand, ma'am, but her daddy ain't white."

Moving right along. Ain't nothing white about my motherfucking baby. I didn't want to break it down to her or let her know about my heritage, my great-grandma's race and how we were cut.

That wasn't any of her goddamn business.

Honestly, at that age I was kind of embarrassed to tell people that I was cut with white and Indian.

I was straight black.

I wasn't about to explain that, but my great-grandma explained to me and my siblings and first cousins our history.

Moving right along with my black baby, she was five shades lighter than me. Four of my siblings were light skinned, I was darker.

My Auntie kids, three were dark skinned, but the fourth was light skinned.

Each one of them had a light-skinned and dark-skinned child.

My grandma, my mother's mother, had two dark-skinned kids and the light-skinned one was my Mama.

By my heritage being how it was, we were mixed colors like that.

I loved the hell out of my daughter. I thanked God for my daughter. I was glad that God gave me a girl. He didn't give me a selfish ass boy.

I felt that boys grow up and disrespect you. No matter how much you give them, love, attention, especially the Mama's boys, those be the main ones that shit on you.

I was blessed to have a girl. The odds were greater for me having a girl than a boy.

I apologize to the men. I wasn't saying that all boys grew up irresponsibly, but the average boys I helped raise, no matter how much I was there for them, they shitted on you.

And the majority of the stories other mothers told me, their sons shitted on them in a minute.

Especially when they get their first piece of tail and didn't know how to handle it.

CHAPTER FIFTEEN
LEARNING MY WAY

MY ONLY CHILD

I was young, and I knew I wasn't ready,
but when I looked into your eyes
I knew at that day and time my life had
changed forever.
The love that you brought to me, the joy that fills
my heart and my spirit
finally feel connected to somebody, a person,
a baby, mine, my baby girl
that I can love, cherish and grow with.
The pain wasn't so hard to bear
when I had so much love to give you, my baby.
A young mother longing to be loved,
now I have this precious soul in my arms
that I can love, I can kiss, I can hug, I can cherish,
I can protect what sat in my stomach
for ten and a half months.
That's mine, all mine's ,
It made me feel free at the moment,
but knowing that I had to go back to the pain,
that hurt where I came from, but at that moment

I know God gave me a gift for a lifetime,
until the end of my life,
and I will always love you!

Your mother,
Lashonta McCray

I was still making bad choices, even though I loved my daughter. I stopped going to Hialeah-Miami Lakes Senior High in the 9th grade.

Fat Boi, my baby daddy, wasn't there for us at all. Biologically, he was a father, but he was still a child and did childish things. He was addicted to his lifestyle. With a newborn baby at home, he still ran the streets, fucked other girls without a care in the world, messed around with my friends, and fucked hos around the 'hood.

Headquarters, his big brother, financially supported me and his niece, my daughter, in the beginning.

He bought clothes and pampers and dropped the items off at my great-grandma's house. I greatly appreciated it. Also, my Pa-Pa and my great-grandma helped take care of my baby.

I stepped up to the plate and took care of my child. Markeisha was a beautiful baby, with light skin like my parents. She was a happy, bow-legged angel that brought joy and cheer to my life, especially during dark times.

My great-grandma told me on Christmas Eve, my baby's birthday, "You're not going to have no more kids."

I always hung out with older cousins and friends. They had their own homes, cars and expensive clothes.

They started putting false stereotypes in my head and I went along with it. I was told that the only way out of the 'hood was by getting a rich nigga, or a nigga with money, or date a big time dope dealer. As a teenager I was running after dudes that had money.

A man that was able to take care of me and my family was gold. I eventually started dating men in their thirties, forties and fifties. Those moneyed sugar daddies picked me up in nice cars, gave me money, and took care of my siblings.

Those men bought my siblings' school clothes, provided food, and helped pay the bills. I enjoyed all the perks that came with dating established men.

Yes, my family knew, but they didn't intervene. Maybe because my great-grandparents, when they were young as me, back in their younger days, as far as my great-grandmothers, they dated older men as well.

So that mentality and way of thinking was passed down through generations until it happened to me.

My mother just didn't give a fuck.

She didn't bring charges up on any of the older men nor did she care to.

Maybe if she broke the generational curse by protecting me from that, if she brought charges against those older men that groomed me, manipulated me into thinking I was doing the right thing in life, then I probably would have made better choices.

Unfortunately, I'd never know. Mama knew better. She never taught me how to do better. Turning a blind eye to my misfortune was her therapy.

My great-grandmother used to be a slave. She even breastfed some of the master's kids. There were many stories my great-grandmother had told me over the years.

She taught me to accept people for who they were. I couldn't judge anyone. She taught me not to be a racist.

When it came to everything going on, compared to what my great-grandmother went through, some people weren't able to stomach some shit the way she had back then.

I wasn't saying everyone was guilty of that, but some people blow things way out of proportion when it came to race issues.

A person could say one harmless word, and suddenly that person was a racist motherfucker. Most of us knew someone who was Spanish or White that grew up with us in the 'Hood. We greet each other as friends. "Yo, what's up dawg, what's up my nigga!" for years.

It was harmless, but in today's society, they were called racist motherfuckers, when they weren't racist at all.

I chose to stay out of it because my great-grandmother used to be a slave. At one point in her life that was her reality.

Chapter Sixteen
Auntie Aretha

Auntie Aretha Bellamy was always humble. She was understanding, she was patient, and she listened to me. She also guided me to the best of her ability. She understood me. She led me down the right path. She tried to understand what I was saying at the time, and if she couldn't understand, or if I didn't explain it right, she was able to guide me.

She was loving and affectionate. She always told me that she loved me. She gave hugs and kisses, affection I wasn't getting from my mother, her sister.

I was 5 ft 8 inches. I was probably the tallest woman on my immediate side of the family. Auntie Aretha was about 5 ft 5, maybe 5 ft 6. She had Indian, curly, wavy hair. My face was shaped like hers, like a pie face.

Auntie Aretha lived with HIV and the stigma and prejudice that came along with it, and it wasn't a good thing. The way she was being treated by certain members of the family and society as a whole broke my heart. I loved her for her, and I always respected her. I didn't treat her any differently. I cared for her all the same.

Auntie loved my daughter and showed her the same love and attention she gave me. She helped fix her bottles and change her diapers.

I didn't know much about HIV, but people were dropping like flies all around me, and around the world from the virus. I was educated about AIDS.

The stereotypes and the stigma was crazy. Rumors swirled around the 'hood that you couldn't drink behind those infected with the virus, and you couldn't eat behind them. At the end of the day, I was a young teenage mother, so I never really cared about what people said.

I loved my Auntie. I ate behind my her. I still let her kiss me on the cheek. I still hugged her; we still showed each other affection.

A lot of people didn't treat her right. Out of all those people, my big brother Vare treated her the worst.

Auntie Aretha had a crack habit, as did most people in the early 80s, including Mama. Auntie and Mama used to steal from my great-grandma Patsy and sold the items for crack.

Auntie was a known thief. She used to steal all types of shit like.

She was one of those masterful thieves that would go in the grocery store and leave out with steaks, filet mignon, you name it.

You couldn't tell she had stolen goods because she wore spanx under her clothes.

When it came to my immediate family, Mama treated her nasty. It was a normal walk in the park for Mama, Charlotte, to treat her younger sister like she didn't matter.

They also had a younger brother, my Uncle. I didn't know him like that. We didn't interact with each other, visit, hang-out, get to know each other. None of the above.

I figured Mama was low-key jealous of my Auntie. She always jumped on her, poked fun at her whether people were around or not.

My big brother treated her like a walking disease. The way he would look at her turned my stomach. The things he would say out of his mouth were uncalled for. I hated the way he disrespected her.

He maneuvered around her like she was toxic, poisonous. He started throwing away everything she ate from, trashed glasses or cups she drank from without a care in the world. He didn't want her lying or sitting on the furniture. He didn't want her lying in the bed. He didn't want her using the towels or the washing rags.

Mind you, he was selling drugs since he was ten years old. When he was twelve, a bong of crack wound up missing. He said that my Auntie stole it.

He burst through the front door, deeply enraged. "Somebody stole my shit! I know it was auntie. She stole my fucking crack!"

There was a dangerous look in his eyes like he wanted to kill somebody. I was terrified for my Auntie. I knew she wouldn't steal from us. Mama never stole from us, either.

They stole my great-grandma's jewelry, her fur coats, and her expensive utensils with her initials on them. They stole expensive shit like that.

Trust me, I wasn't justifying their actions. Later on, I saw my auntie holding her head as she came around the corner, with blood gushing out.

Savagely, my big brother walked slowly behind her with a pistol. It was like the spin gun the famous cowboy John Wayne had, and I'd been watching John Wayne since I was a little girl.

"Where's my drugs?"

"It wasn't me; I swear!"

"Stop lying, auntie! I know it was you that stole my crack! Now where my shit at?"

"I promise you, nephew! I would never steal from you. I did not take your crack."

Heartbroken and fearing her life, she was crying profusely.

My Auntie was sobbing, with blood pouring from her head. I called 9-1-1.

Angrily, I glared at my brother. "I'm putting your ass in jail!"

When the police arrived, they arrested him and took him to juvie, since he was a minor. I really didn't know if the cops let him go, or if they took him in. That was up in the air.

To add insult to injury, I heard that he found the crack in the house he accused my auntie of stealing. My auntie was telling the truth.

He never apologized to her for falsely accusing her of missing dope he misplaced, and he didn't apologize for pistol whipping her.

Even after that, my auntie remained loving and loyal, and he still treated her like shit. It really pissed me the fuck off. I was mad because she didn't deserve that. It didn't matter if she was on drugs, or had HIV, she was our only auntie. That was Mama's only sister.

My brother was cold-hearted, to the core. He lived in that truth, and it wasn't easy to deal with or tolerate. Honestly, my brother never stayed with us. He was like our Mama, she never stayed with her Mama.

When Mama was born, she was brought home from the hospital and lived with her grandma.

In fact, when Vare was born, he went straight to my great-grandma. All he knew was great-grandma's house, which was his home, not Mama's. So, he never lived with our Mama.

Unlike me, I didn't move with my great-grandma Patsy until I was five years old, after my dad went to prison on a robbery bid.

Mama brought me to live with her after I was born.

And it's crazy, I wouldn't say it's crazy, but when my aunt Aretha died, she left behind a baby daughter. She didn't remember her mom, but she carried on her mother's name and memory.

Auntie Aretha's daughter wasn't even two years old yet when her mother passed away. Come to think of it, she was 2 years old because my daughter was only a few months old.

Those two right there, my daughter and my first cousin, we're very close. They were like sisters.

You would think that both of them had the same mom and the same dad. It was so beautiful to me how close they were.

If it was a possibility, I know that when the dead were dead, they were dead, I was raised that way.

They didn't see anything, they weren't helping with anything, they couldn't give you any blessings. They were dead.

I knew that, but I had to believe in my heart that my auntie Aretha was smiling down on their special relationship.

CHAPTER SEVENTEEN
SPOILED

Great-grandma Patsy paid all of our bills. She paid Mama's rent like clockwork, she paid for all of Mama's cars, and bought all of our groceries.

I couldn't recall my mother ever working for anything. My great-grandma was her financial security.

She was a spoiled fucking brat. She never had to work for anything. Everything was given to her.

I didn't think my great-grandma paid my mother's way as a means to hinder her, even though that was how an outsider may see it. She still had a slave mentality.

She used to be a slave, in every sense of the word and its bloody history. She grew accustomed to doing everything on her own without much help from anyone.

My mom was her blood granddaughter. Out of all the kids there, Mama was her only blood descendant. The rest were foster kids my great grandma was paid by the state to take care of.

She raised hundreds of foster children. She wasn't a strict disciplinarian.

In a way that was a hinderance because Mama wasn't taught normal, everyday things.

They didn't have chores. In a normal household, the parents taught the child how to sweep, mop, do laundry, iron clothes, cook, make up the bed, and clean up behind themselves.

My great-grandma did everything, with a slave mentality.

Mama and the foster kids didn't have to lift a finger. Neither did me and my siblings. She did it all for us.

She even bathed us up until a respectable age. Scrubbed our bodies for us, literally.

It only hindered me because I learned how to fend for myself and take care of myself and learn those things in the streets.

My grandma Lily on my dad's side showed me certain self-efficient things, but she didn't teach me how to fold a shirt or pour bleach in the dishwater.

I did have little minor chores because she was a very organized, clean woman.

I got part of my OCD from her. We couldn't have anything on the tables or the floor.

Everything in her house had its place and that was the way it had to be, or else.

I couldn't put anything on the bed or the furniture. This woman's house had to be immaculate. No ifs, and or but's about it.

She had rules, unlike great grandma Patsy. You mess it up, you clean it up. I knew not to talk back. I had to do what I was told.

I had to go to school. My siblings and I ate three times a day when we visited.

One rule I absolutely hated, and it might seem petty, but she would not let us drink anything until we ate all of our food.

I was too scared to ask her why. Asking why would get me fucked up, so I knew better.

Hell, grandma still jumped on her grown children, and she was a tiny woman.

She weighed about one hundred pounds, that was how skinny she was, soaked and wet.

I was terrified of my grandma.

I had an older cousin named Keyda.

She was like a big sister. We'd been through a lot.

From the time I was an adolescent until now, there was a lot I learned from her, and all of it wasn't good.

Mind you she was about seven years older than me, so when I had my daughter, I automatically thought I was on her level of thinking and living.

She was a grown woman. I was a teenager. The good things she taught me turned out to be bad things.

I loved the fact that she let me be around her, to see how she navigated through life. Even though I was a mother, my dad's side of the family still didn't let me do what I wanted to do.

The only time I could go anywhere was with my cousin.

I clung to her out of everybody I dealt with on a daily basis.

Chapter Eighteen
Robbing

As I sit and reflect, I think about all the years of scamming, scheming, gold-digging, robbing and stripping. I remember me, my little sister, her baby daddy, and a few of his friends that I've known since we were much younger started getting into mischief.

We were too grown. Pretty fast, if you asked me. We stopped going to school. We ran the streets like there was no tomorrow. We truly lived in the moment, no matter how destructive it was.

I didn't know what made us pick up robbing people as a hobby. Oh, yea. I remembered now. One of my brothers, Al, and Tee, was already robbing folks. Not to mention my dad was locked up for the same offense I was curious about. The irony was astounding.

My brother, Al, told us stories about getting expensive jewelry and fast money. It was a quick come up that became an addiction.

Al put the entire scheme together, that introduced me and my sister into robbing.

The way his mind worked was something else. I soaked up all the game like a sponge.

All the bois were handsome (Al, Tee and their homeboi).

The ladies, me included, were some bad chicks. We looked good, too. Starting out, me and my sister were doing it before my two cousins, Yaya and Wanna, joined in on the action.

We were so clever we'd research potential areas before we did anything. Developed a route and a plan. We'd be in a stolen car as we go to moneyed locations. Uppity areas.

We'd cruise around until we saw a potential victim. We'd ride past her, scope out the area, map out a route of escape, then we determined where we were going to park at.

Finally, one of the bois would rob the victim.

Our technique was simple. The bois used their handsome looks to win over their prey.

We'd see a girl with a bunch of jewelry walking alone, or if she carried an expensive purse or if she drove a flashy car, that was even better.

One of the bois would hop out of the stolen ride and approach her. Just one of the bois, so they didn't make it obvious. He sweet talk her until he won her over. He'd get her number if he had to. She dropped her guard after thinking he was interested in dating her.

She was under the assumption that a fine nigga tried to talk to her, yet we were parked a few blocks away, waiting to act.

Abruptly, he took her for what she had. Her wallet, purse, jewelry, money, everything. We showed no mercy.

Some things I wouldn't say or repeat.

That's how we financed our living arrangements. We were literally living from hotel to motel. We'd get older people to rent the room for us.

We were teens, ages ranged from fifteen to seventeen, living like this. It was a phase I had to endure.

At this time, I started wearing name brand tennis shoes, name brand designer clothes. I was not saying that I was trying to dress like a boy. I'd been wearing four inch heels since I was thirteen. This was my sneaker phase, which was short-lived.

Tennis shoes were not my forte.

Even though at sixteen I'd started robbing bitches, I was already heavy on the adult scene. I did my thing. I was mixing it up and vibing with different crowds. I was clubbing, baby.

However, I couldn't fully get into the club scene because I had a three year old daughter. I didn't know which way I wanted to go in life. I just wanted to have fun and look good doing it. I seldom thought of the consequences.

I lost my great-granddaddy, Pa-pa, at sixteen. There was a lot going on with me mentally. Guilt and regret rode me like a bad dream.

I didn't get to apologize to my great-granddaddy for all the wrong I did. The fucked up shit I said was unforgivable. Things I could never take back. Things he'd never physically hear me acknowledge.

That got to me.

A few weeks later we went into an area that was quiet and low on crime, looking for a quick come up. Hialeah had predominately Spanish people.

We were riding around in an old ass Cadillac. I didn't think the car was stolen this time.

I say that because my brothers were a bunch of gigolos. I wasn't going to lie. The older women they talked to had their own cars, houses and apartments. If I was not mistaken, I could be wrong, Al borrowed somebody's car. It belonged to one of the dudes one of my cousins dated.

I guessed we looked suspicious because a police squad car got behind us. Oh, shit. We were minors. Neither one of us had a valid driver's license.

With nothing to lose, Al mashed on the gas pedal and led the police on a high speed chase. We got away! We lost the police!

Then bam! A loud noise came from out of nowhere as my head hit the dashboard.

Disoriented, I looked up and noticed that both of my brothers, Al and Nard, had jumped out of the crashed vehicle, and ran away. Shit, so I jumped out and started running away, too.

We were on the other side of Amelia Earhart Park.

When we got far enough away, we stopped running to catch our breath. Just then a police squad came up the block from the opposite way, in our direction.

Instantly, Al ducked behind a big bolo rock that was in the corner of a stranger's yard used as decoration.

There was no fence.

Me and my brother Nard, continued to walk up the block.

Keeping his cool, Nard glanced at me. "Listen. We're going to pretend that we're a couple," he said to me, and I nodded. That's how quickly we were able to come up with an escape plan since Al was still hiding behind the bolo rock.

As expected, the police stopped us.

"Where's your I.D?" he asked us with venom in his voice.

We didn't have identification.

"What's your names and date of birth."

Each of us gave him the necessary info.

He gave us the side eye. "You're the ones that jumped out of that car we were chasing."

We denied it vehemently, keeping our reserve. I was too bitter to be scared, but I knew that if I gave anything away, we'd be fucked.

They weren't too convinced.

"Yes you are!" He said more sternly.

"Whhaatttt? We don't know what you're talking about! We just came from Amelia Air Park. We're walking back home. We live in Opa-Locka," I said, looking him in the face.

He frowned. "Yea, yea, yea...save it. All of you jumped outta that damn car."

We stuck to our story. They didn't have proof that we jumped out that old ass Cadillac. There was no one around when we abandoned the car.

I glanced behind them and saw Al still hiding behind the bolo rock.

The cops arrested us. I was so nervous. Inside, I was a wreck. This was not how the plan was supposed to go. We were supposed to rob a bitch and slide. Nowhere in that plan did I imagine being in a squad car.

They took us to the police station. I didn't know if it was the Hialeah station or not, but the funniest thing happened.

The station was so country.

A big light up pig head emblem was on the wall. There was a huge table with wooden benches on either side.

"Oh, Lord...they have a Porky's bar in this bitch!" I said, chuckling. Literally. I thought it was freaking hilarious! Nard and I was cracking up!

I thought about Al and the smile died from my face. We didn't know what the cops did with him.

Shit, my bad. I take it back. Al got away! That little, short motherfucker was lucky as shit! The cops didn't see him. We never said anything. We kept Al a secret. The cops overlooked him.

While Al was squatting behind the bolo rock that was taller than his short ass, they drove right past him.

After some time went by, we were joking, talking, and ranking on people while the cops called our parents.

Fortunately for us, they couldn't hold us, keep us in custody or charge us with anything.

They had no proof that we were in the abandoned Cadillac nor were there any witnesses.

The cops separated us for questioning, and we still stuck to our stories. They tried to manipulate us into snitching on each other.

Cop glared at me. "Are you sure you're not one of the high speed chase candidates?"

"I don't know what you're talking about."

"Well, Nard says differently."

"I don't know what you're talking about. "

"We got evidence that you were in that Cadillac."

"I don't know what you're talking about."

"Your boyfriend said you were the driver."

"I don't know what you're talking about."

We were intelligent. We knew the code of the streets. You didn't know anything. You didn't say shit. You didn't volunteer information. Lie to those motherfuckers. Fake it till you made it.

Even if the cops lied to us and say one said something in private about the other, stick to the damn script.

"I don't know what you're talking about."

Nothing more. Nothing less.

Do not bend or fold. We were already hip to survival type of shit. We couldn't be manipulated.

That's how it was in the early nineties. Cops played reverse psychology games, but it didn't work. We didn't give a damn how many times they say one snitched on the other.

We knew the drill. We knew the routine. We knew that we trusted each other, and we'd never rat each other out.

They let us go. They took off the handcuffs. We were together as a group again, minus Al.

No money.

No jewelry.

No quick come up.

No charges.

Our parents arrived and took us home.

My Pa-Pa, a World War II veteran, came to pick me up. I left Nard behind. Pa-pa didn't beat or spank me. He didn't curse me out or demean me or made me feel any worse than I already felt.

He wasn't the emotional type. He was born in 1909, so his upbringing was a bit different from the shit I had to deal with. We never had to say please or thank you.

Hell, I never even had to clean my own room, I never had to wash clothes or cook because my great-grandmother did all of that for us. After I had my daughter, shit, I didn't even have to come home like other kids.

I stopped getting whippings after I had my baby. No, my Pop didn't like it, but great-grandma had her own mind.

As he drove, he said, "Now you know better."

We were lucky, but that luck would blow up in our face in the weeks to come.

Al and Nard always told me that if we ever get caught, I was always the girl offered a ride home. I always stuck to my story and cops had to prove otherwise.

Ninety percent of the time it worked, yet there was always that one time that it didn't.

We were in the Norland area, which was off of 183rd and 17th Avenue.

We saw a guy walking. He had on two expensive necklaces.

When it's a male victim, there was no Mack daddy talk or phone number exchanging. We quietly assessed him, scoped the area, found an exit route once the deal was sealed and we parked.

Normally, Nard or Al would act like they was going to pass him. They would pull the fire on him. *"Give it up!"*, but we didn't have a gun this time.

I was letting you know something serious. This ain't *Little House on the Prairie* in *Mr. Roger's neighborhood*. This was real life for me at the time.

If victims tried to buck, they were hit or shot. Guaranteed. Good thing no one tried to run off or put up a fight.

Wasting no time, Al's short, cocky ass jumped out and ran at the tall stocky dude.

Startled, the dude didn't know whether to squat or piss. Al meant business. "Come up off this shit, nigga!"

Al grabbed ole boi and muscled the chains from his neck. Once the chains were secure, Al bucked off. Once he got to the car, he hopped inside. The adrenaline was so high you could cut it with a knife.

We drove by him. Mind you ole boi didn't know that we were the mothafuckahs that robbed him. He was looking lost as fuck.

I looked the dude in the face. A jolt shot through my body. Oh, no. He was a dude I went to school with. I was like, "Oh my God!"

As we drove off, I couldn't hold back the words.

"You just robbed my classmate, bra."

"Word, shid, how was I supposed to know."

"He's cool as fuck, tho! Like for real, for real."

"Fuck that shit," said Nard. "He got, got nah!"

Of course, I wasn't going to say his name.

All I could say was that he attended North Dade Middle School.

CHAPTER NINETEEN:
ANOTHER STOLEN CAR

As I continued to reflect on my robbing phase, I meditate. It all played out in my mind, my selfish acts. I didn't know where me and the crew were coming from, but in this instance, since I was never caught, I was omitting the location or any clues so there was nothing to figure out.

Truth be told, we got away with a lot of things that could've ended badly had we been caught.

In that we became bolder and cockier. We were smelling ourselves. Robbing was the choice. We truly didn't give a fuck. It was all or nothing. There was no in between.

In another stolen car, me, Al, Dan and Nard were cruising through an area by Opa-Locka, driving pretty fast. There were two dudes walking, talking and minding their business in the middle of the street.

We were not too far from Bunch Park. We were headed back to the Miami Inn. I couldn't really make out what they were wearing, but one of them had on a white T-shirt.

Frustrated, Al started blowing the horn, hoping they would move out of the way.

Honk! Honk!

"Get y'all asses outta the road!" Al shouted.

They didn't. They kept gaslighting the shit they were talking, getting us angrier by the second.

Defensively, Al guided the car to the left a bit to keep from hitting them.

Grittily, Dan said, "I'll shoot those mothafuckahs!"

"Shoot 'em then, fuck it!" I encouraged.

Dan opened the back door and shot at them...

They flipped the middle finger at us, still talking shit like they were about that life.

They had no idea that we were a bunch of rebellious teens who did not give a fuck about nothing in life in that moment.

I wasn't saying that I didn't love my daughter. My mentality was in I-didn't-care mode.

"I know that fuck nigga ain't shoot at me," one of the dudes said in disbelief, the one that wore the white T-shirt. The dude was angrier. I know if somebody was shooting at me, I wasn't gonna talk shit to enrage the gun man any further, but those guys were different.

My brother looked back, laughing. It was an evil sounding laugh that caught my attention. His eyes were different, more sinister. Hell, we all were laughing with the same energy.

"Is this fuck nigga serious? I shot at him, stared at this nigga…"

Hell, I was offended. "For real," I agreed. "This bitch is bold!"

Al frowned. "I know those fuck niggas ain't talking shit!"

Before Al could stop the car, Dan opened the door. "What you said nah, fuck nigga?"

One of the dudes said, "Don't worry 'bout it muthafuckah!"

"These niggas still talking shit? I'm about to shoot at your fuck ass again!"

"That's right pussy ass niggas. Buss his ass, brother," I yelled, agreeing with him. We switched sides because Dan wanted a better angle than the first time. Dan leaned back out of the car. Let one off. Pow.

He didn't shoot at them to cause harm, but in a way that intimidated them. Only it did the opposite.

The nigga's white T-shirt became red in an instant. Oh, shit! My brother actually shot his ass.

"Drive, nigga…drive!" Dan yelled as Al mashed on the gas pedal. We hauled ass. "Talk that shit nah!"

"We gotta lay low, y'all!" I said.

"Shit, shit, shit why did you have to shoot the nigga?" I chimed. We laughed and joked, thinking of the next plan to come up on some money.

Before I knew it, Al sped into the Miami Inn parking lot. Once we conned some lame ass Cuban to rent the room for us, we ditched him, and we locked ourselves inside and got high as fuck.

We joked and laughed about the ordeal like we were watching an urban comedy.

That fuck nigga brought wrath on himself, did all of that on his own.

Part of me knew better, that we were being too careless in our actions.

Yet I didn't care. At all.

I was familiar with this particular hotel. I once had my first party out here when I was fifteen in Meadow Groove at my grandma Lily's house. A party that brought me closer to my brothers, especially Al.

Baby, I had the whole block on swole. "Swole," in the south means packed with people. It was thick and lit before lit was a thing. Some of every-fucking-body showed up. Even my mind was blown. Who knew that I'd throw the party of the century.

Me and my cousin Pookie's party was one for the books.

Of course, my cousin had to lie to my grandmother Lily for me. He used his birthday as an alibi to disguise that it was really a party for me, or else she wouldn't have allowed it.

I was the popular one.

Once the block party concluded, it was time for the damn after party at the Miami Inn.

Yes, I was fifteen throwing a lit after party.

I brought the hotel a lot of business.

We had three floors on lock, partying. I didn't know that many people would follow me to the hotel. I didn't know that I was that popular.

So many people rented rooms and all. I enjoyed myself. I partied like it was 1999, Prince style.

When you walked off the elevator you could see thick clouds of weed smoke dancing up the hallways.

I was like what the fuck.

It was ironic that one of the maintenance men from a previous job of mine was on FB, looking at my old pictures.

He hit me up.

He attended my party from that era in my life, but we didn't know each other at the time.

Hold up. Are you Shante from Opa Locka? He wrote.

Yea, I responded.

I didn't recognize you because you didn't have your gold grills. Yo, I remember when I first met you, you had a party when we were teenagers in Meadow Grove! I was with my dawg, Tee.

Tee was my boyfriend at the time; somebody I called myself being in love with. Puppy dog shit.

The party was legendary, but my future was anything but. From that point on, for me, the Miami Inn and Motel 7 were the main motels we hung out at.

When we successfully got money, we chilled there. It was special to me, those beautiful times.

Unfortunately, beautiful times didn't always last for long.

CHAPTER TWENTY:
FIRST TIME

The time came for me to do my first robbery. Up until that point, Nard and Al usually robbed people while I stayed in the getaway car, but that changed when it was my turn to put up or shut up. Was I up for the challenge? Of course I was, but part of me opposed it.

Put up. Or shut up. I jumped out on a come-up by myself, without a gun and tried to rob them.

I wasn't as vicious as my brother, but I was the bitch you didn't want to cross, unless you were on a suicide mission.

I go after what I wanted and didn't stop until I had it.

I wasn't going to say too much about my first jump-out robbery. I wasn't going to incriminate myself, so I'd say "allegedly."

My first two potential candidates fell into my lap. I say that because me and my crew were just passing through the neighborhood, chilling in another stolen car, of course.

When we spotted our potential victims walking on the main avenue, Nard and Al looked them over.

Once the assessment was done, we checked out the area and looked for somewhere to park.

But there was a problem. We parked too far away from the come-up, by a church of all places. There were no corners, just a long ass street.

I had a lot of running to do. A *long* run down a popular main avenue, at that! That was some bold shit.

I wasn't having it at first. I glared at my brothers. Hell, I didn't even recall them having to run this far to rob a bitch. Why did my first lick have to be with the shits?

"*Gahdamn!* Is this the closest y'all can park? The come-up is on the main avenue, bra!"

My heart was racing, but I had no fear. I wasn't scared, just anxious for the win. I was too excited.

Come on! Get that money! Fuck it. Let's get it!

I hopped out. Nervously, I walked slowly at first. After my confidence grew, I'd run, then slow up so I didn't bring attention on myself. I was speed walking, then walking regularly. I didn't want to scare off the elderly couple, my potential come-up.

I didn't expect a couple like this to be out around this time. Plus, the location wasn't an uppity area filled with wealthy people, like in expensive ass Aventura.

I didn't remember exactly what part of Miami we were, but the residents of the area were well off.

As for the elderly couple, now in my view and on my radar, they looked out of place, like they didn't belong in this part of town.

That's what stuck out to me like a sore thumb.

The closer I got to them I was amping myself up; I was mentally preparing myself to snatch the old lady's purse. My plan was simple. I had a strategy. I wasn't going to snatch the purse forward. Because where my crew was parked at, there was no way I could run back that way unless I wanted to get caught.

But if I pulled the purse backward, I'd have great success. I could snatch and run and catch up with my crew later.

Get it! Abruptly, I grabbed and snatched her purse. Yes! I got it...

Oh, shit! This old lady wasn't letting go of her purse. As she yelled and shouted on the popular main avenue, she was drawing attention to us.

I was cold inside. Mentally, it didn't click in my head that this wasn't right, but I didn't give a fuck. I was heartless. I was cold. I didn't care if I lived or died, not to say that I was suicidal. I wasn't into self- harm. I didn't have a conscious. I didn't fear death. Jail or hell, I honestly didn't give a fuck. I feel so shitty.

She had a death grip on the purse. I yanked it and her screaming ass to the ground.

She wouldn't let her purse go. Not only did I have the purse, but I was also dragging her down the Avenue.

The elderly man ran at me trying to help her.

I had so much hurt, pain and anger built up in me. From age six to that moment, I felt invincible and invisible.

I finally snagged her purse. Feeling victorious, I caught out running towards the car, down that long ass street.

Once I hopped inside the get-away car, Al drove off. We got away. Mission accomplished. Didn't go the way I planned it, but the purse and all the money and the wallet, ID, house keys and all was in my lap. My hands itched just thinking about it.

"You did that shit! You got the bag!" Nard said excitedly.

I opened the purse.

My heart and confidence dropped.

It was empty inside.

Chapter Twenty-One: I'm done robbing

I felt shitty. I went through hell fighting for an empty purse. I put the elderly woman through hell taking her purse. And she fought me for dear life, even put her life on the line for *an empty purse!*

What if I had ended her when she first resisted? I'd have blood on my hands over *an empty purse.* They say be careful about what you ask for. I wanted a purse, that's what I ended up with.

An empty motherfucking purse with two dollars and some change and her credentials. I was deep in my pride and ego about this shit. My feelings would never be the same.

You know how embarrassing that was. Wow, what a shitty turn of events.

All that running up that long ass street still gave me chills. I knew this might anger a lot of people with this revelation.

I truly apologize in advance. This was my story. I was giving it blood raw.

Trust me. I was angry at myself for my transgressions. I was not in the right frame of mind. I was ruled by emotional damage.

Deeply bothered, my crew and I cruised along. We cut our losses and moved on.

That was a major "L". (Loss).

A few short miles away we targeted another area, our initial targeted area, before we changed our minds and wound up on the main avenue.

In no time I saw a black Haitian lady. Maybe she was a foreigner, who knew. We never targeted people based on their race or ethnicity.

Financially stable people were our victims. I wanted to elaborate a bit more. In the 'hood, niggas always justified robbing people by saying, "At least they weren't black!"

Bitch, robbing was robbing. As long as we get the bag, we were good.

This area had blocks everywhere, so there were better escape routes. Shorter distances to run.

I jumped out of the stolen car and snatched her purse. It was as sweet as cake. Once I grabbed it, I hopped back in the car, and we got away.

I felt a sense of victory. I just knew she had to have valuables in this pricey purse. Anxiously, I checked the contents.

This bitch was no better than the elderly woman. The purse didn't have shit in it, not even lint.

There was only a few foreign bills in the pocket, worthless shit. *Fuck! Not again!*

All that shit was for nothing.

This was America. What the fuck was foreign money going to do for me?

Those foreign dollars probably had sentimental value to that lady. I took it away in search of the big cash come up and came up

embarrassingly short the first two times I jumped
out of stolen cars.

At that point in my life, I was coming to the
end of my robbery phase. It was not what I thought
it would be.

At the end of the day, no matter what I did, or
how it started and ended, I was still a teenage
mother, and my daughter should come first.

I knew that hitting licks and robbing people
wasn't for me any longer. The thrill was gone.

I could've wound up dead or incarcerated like
my father for doing the same shit I wound up
doing.

Reality kicked in and I quit robbing people all
together. It was one of the best decisions of my life.

My brothers inevitably started going to prison
for twelve and fifteen years, repeating a
dysfunctional cycle my father should have broken.

I was blessed to still have my freedom.

Another experience with a stolen car. I was 15
years old. It was me, Al, and my friend. We were in
a stolen car, looking for a stolen car.

We were in another seedy, high-class area of
Miami. A place we didn't belong. A place where
people had money.

I was on the passenger side. Al was the one
who jumped out this time. My friend stayed in the
car with me.

We were on the lookout. Nice apartment
buildings were all around us.

Al attempted to steal the car. My friend tapped
me with a concerned look on his face. He said, "I

think somebody is peeping out the window, looking at us."

Cautiously, I looked at the window. I stared at it. The curtain opened again.

"Yo, Al! Come on, man! Somebody is looking at you!"

"I almost got it!" Al said.

"Man come on! Somebody looking at us bra!"

Al was so fucking hard-headed. He ignored us and stayed focused. He refused to leave. It was all or nothing at this point.

He was almost finished with jacking the car.

My brother used to have a master key to a LE Camry and a pulley. He was quite experienced and good at what he did, with no fear in his heart.

I didn't know what was holding him up, but whatever it was it made it longer for him to nab the car. I pleaded with my brother to leave, and he still was trying to steal the car.

Next thing I knew the police pulled up behind us and my heart dropped.

Mind you we were already in a stolen car and was caught trying to steal another car.

The police arrested us. They asked me what I was doing there. I told them I was getting a ride home.

That was my story and I stuck to it, got-damnit. To my dismay we were taken to the Miami Lakes Police Station for further questioning. Had Al listened to us we wouldn't be in this shit. We would still be out there getting money.

We couldn't make shit if we were handcuffed in the back of a police car.

We all had a bond. If we were ever separated by the authorities, we wouldn't tell them shit. No matter how they tried to mind fuck us by saying one of us blew the whistle, we didn't snitch. We knew their routine. We already knew what to do.

I was put in a room; Al was put in another room and my friend was put in one room. As predicted, they separated us. We were apart for hours. It seemed like an eternity.

I didn't know what to think. I knew to keep my mouth shut. Nobody seen anything.

After an eternity I finally got to see one of my brothers, Al. We were handcuffed from behind, sitting next to each other on the floor.

Our friend, I wasn't going to say his name, was still talking to the cops. For a long time, he was with them. I glanced at Al.

"Nah, bra. This is taking too long. If we all stuck to our story one or two things would have already happened. We would be on the way to the juvenile detention center, or we'd be released by now."

Nine times out of ten they wouldn't have taken our black asses to juvenile. We would just have to show up for court.

Al said, "This bitch in there snitching on us."

"Shut that shit up nah. Our friend ain't talkin' to the cops. He ain't no snitch. We don't rock like that."

"I'm trying to tell you, sis. He snitched. They got us handcuffed out here and he still in there talking to the cops?"

I'd be damned.

Our friend surely did snitch. Even though we weren't charged or convicted of car theft, the cops actually told us that our friend told them everything.

TWENTY-TWO:
THE SNITCH

He was a singing canary. Our friend didn't know, until this day, that we knew he ratted us out. We never told his snitching ass. We just knew, going forward, that we couldn't move with him like that anymore.

Don't get me wrong, that same friend I loved right now today, but you snitched on us, nigga. And the cops snitched on you after you snitched on us.

Again, I couldn't say his name because he was a part of Myrtle Grove Park and they'd be like what the fuck.

You snitched? My brother Al knew who I was talking about. I love my friend, but we know you snitched on us. Without a doubt.

Pa-Pa had to come get me again from another police department. That was my second time being arrested in a stolen car.

The third time I got arrested I didn't even know I was in a stolen car.

Alright, there was this dude named Sammy. Anybody from Opa-Locka knew Sammy.

Sammy was supposedly a relative or somebody close to my baby daddy's side of the family.

That unfortunate day it was me and my baby daddy's sister named Bay. I didn't know who else was with us, I really couldn't remember.

He came up to us. After a few beats of silence, he said, "*Yooo*, I'm about to take y'all out show you all the good time. We're going to Red Lobster. I came up on a huge lick..."

I gazed at him. Because if anybody knew Sammy, they knew how he made his money.

What was understood didn't need to be explained when it came to that.

Shit, we were game! Red Lobster on your tab? *Hell yeah!*

Bay and I was on board. I said, "Alright, alright. I'm with it. I'll go."

So, me and Bay hopped in Sammy's car. He had a bad ass ride. We drove to Carol City. We were living it up. We were feeling ourselves.

We were really going to Red Lobster.

We were seen around the 'hood in Sammy's car. He was a go-getter type of nigga that knew how to get money.

He could have had a car filled with hoes, he could have had his bois with him, but he gave me and Bay the keys to the whip so we could enjoy ourselves in his car.

CHAPTER TWENTY-THREE:
NEVER AGAIN

ay asked me stop by some nigga name Scooby's house in the Myrtle Grove Park area. Everybody used to be crazy about him. God rest his soul because later on he was killed, or he drowned or something like that.

After we left there, we drove up on my sister Tie's second baby daddy, Nard.

He started flagging us down when he saw us.

He shouted, "Aye, aye, aye! Wassup! Let a nigga get a ride, shit!"

We weren't trying to hear it. Girls' day out. We were on a mission, minding our business.

"Man, we're about to go somewhere."

He didn't listen. He got in the car. We didn't know that this muthafuckah just got in trouble with the law and he was running from the police.

That was probably why he didn't tell us why he needed a ride.

To my dismay, the police pulled up behind us. Just like a nigga to spoil our plans. I wanted some Red Lobster. He was taken into custody; I was also arrested along with Bay.

Did you know why I was arrested? Drum roll, please: I was driving a stolen car.

No wonder Sammy let us drive it, so the shit fell on me and Bay while his nose stayed clean. Set our asses up.

If that wasn't the case Sammy would have told us that the bitch was stolen. He had the key to it because he took it from somebody.

We were ridin' dirty and got busted. There weren't any signs that the car was stolen.

The dashboard was intact, he gave us a key to the car. I was stunned and upset.

I should have known that nothing was free and a nigga never gave you a dime or did shit for you without an agenda.

I wondered if we would have drove right past Nard and stuck to our dinner outing, we probably would still be free.

Too late for wishful thinking now. I could choke Nard's hard-headed ass.

Of course, we kept Sammy's name out of it. We didn't reveal who gave us the car, but I did say I got the key from someone I didn't know to keep a cover.

Not only that, the cops gave me a ticket for driving without a license, but they had the nerve to give me a ticket for a broken headlight and it wasn't even my car! The nerve! You petty sons of bitches!

I was illiterate to the law because of the ignorance of my age. I didn't know that if you drove someone else's car that you were responsible for it, so that was a legit ticket. I also didn't know that those tickets would sit and gain interest on my record.

What pissed me off the most was the fact that I was literally arrested when I wasn't up to no good. All the stolen cars I was in, and I never got arrested in them, and I go out to eat in Sammy's alleged car and boom, jail, bitch!

How ironic. They said that karma was a bitch. Trust me, she was a bitch. Sometime later I encountered a dude named Frank. He was a little older, but he was a teen like me. He lived in the Norland area.

He wanted to be a down dude. My brothers and those associated with me knew him or knew of him.

He was a spoiled brat, and his mother was never home to watch, guard or supervise him. Which made him fair game with unlimited possibilities. He lived in a nice, big house.

Once we were acquainted, me and my crew started hanging out at his crib. Oh my. It was like the Lifestyle of the Rich and Famous in that bitch.

Living a life of abundance and luxury compared to where I lived and where I was from became goals.

Hell, I didn't want to leave at that moment. I could see myself having that kind of life, buying nice clothes and nice things.

His mother had to be loaded to afford this fancy ass house. The layout was gold and black. He had a see-through toilet seat with money in it,

blankets made from Polo and Nautica, and a
plethora of expensive shit all over the dam place.

Throughout the house were expensive
televisions; there was a TV in the bathrooms, the
den, the bedrooms, the patio, and the kitchen.

I could not wrap my mind around his
mother's beautiful home. Wow, like any girl in the
world would love to acquire a home like this.

There were golden statues, ceramic panthers
that shined in the dim lighting like diamonds.

Who knew black folk could have something so
exquisite.

I wasn't going to mince words, but Frank tried
to be a down-ass dude, having all kinds of people
in and out of his mother's house, including the
company we brought.

It got to a point where my brother Al stopped
people that wasn't in our crew from coming over
and took over the boy's house. Those that were
hanging out before we got there Al kicked them all
out after snapping on them. "Yo, get y'all asses
out! Ya'll ain't cleaning shit, y'all ain't cooking,
y'all are breaking shit, y'all got to get the fuck out."

After we came over in the days to come,
nobody was allowed inside Frank's house except
for me, Frank, Yaya, Wanna, Al, Nard, Tie, her
baby daddy, and my brother-in-law. Frank's house
was our new meeting place and our hangout spot.
We could go make money robbing people and
didn't have to ask an adult to get a hotel for us.

We felt independent. We weren't in school or

anything, we never really went home. We went straight to Frank's house.

Each of us had our own room. It became our house. Frank was a good person. He looked out for us. He truly had a good heart.

Wanna and I decided to date niggas outside of our group. I didn't date niggas that knew my brothers or those closest to me.

Out of the blue, I didn't know what happened, but one of my people said they were burning, meaning somebody caught a venereal disease.

We all went down to the health department as fifteen and sixteen years old. The officials really didn't give a shit if our parents were with us or not.

The way everybody acted when we arrived made me laugh, even though being burned was no joking matter. Al was on the floor under one of the seats.

We told the officials that two people from my crew on two different occasions said that something wasn't right with their bodies.

Because of that information it was recommended that we all had to get immunization shots in our asses.

I swore I heard a record scratch somewhere.

I was pissed. "Why we have to all get a dam shot...?"

"You all said that you were being reckless. And you all hang out together," said the official.

"But we all had nothing to do with being burned. And before you think it, we do not fuck each other. I don't sleep with friends or cousins, that's not how I get down."

But since the health department officials viewed us as irresponsible teenagers, and we were all fifteen and sixteen years old, they gave us all the shots whether we wanted it or not.

I didn't enjoy that experience at all. "What's in that shot?" I asked, fumed. I thought they said penicillin or something, who knew.

We were mad as fuck.

CHAPTER TWENTY-FOUR
I LOVE BOWLEGS: MY TEENAGE CRUSH

I didn't understand the anger that surged through me from all of us having to get a shot. Who knew that being a teenager, living your life feeling like you're invincible, would lead to the moment of a needle going in my ass. And Lord knows, it hurt like a bitch. I never imagined that type of consequence for somebody else's mistake.

There was a throbbing sensation after she pulled the needle out that lingered on my ass cheek for nearly the rest of the day. It was sore for me to sit down.

Once we received our results, we were all disease free. None of us was burned, thank God. So, the person in the group that cried that he was burned with an STD must have been false or else one of a few of us would have been positive.

One thing was for sure, when we left the facility, we each had a small paper bag filled with condoms in our possession.

We made sure we were going to protect ourselves by having safe sex as we moved forward.

That incident would scare anybody straight, especially if one of us had a disease that didn't have a cure.

We went back to Frank's house. The crew started cleaning up the place. I cooked for us. I barely knew what to do.

I took that back. I didn't cook a dam thing. I once tried to cook an egg, but that shit burnt.

We usually ate takeout. Going to places that was quick to grab something to eat and stay on the go. Papa John's was our absolute favorite place to eat.

One thing was for sure, we were some pizza eating ass teenagers. Pizza, pizza damn pizza.

I didn't know when the jealousy thing started, but it did. One summer day, it was hot as hell too, we were hustling. We were all out in the streets getting our bag the best way we could. Wanna and I was always up to no good.

We made a pit stop to get some money from some dudes before we headed back to Frank's house.

But when we all got back to the house, the hangout spot, the door was locked. We knocked and nobody answered. We knocked and knocked and knocked. Nothing.

We found that weird. My sister, Tie, was about to act a fool.

She looked at us and said, "Yo, why are they not opening the door? They're tripping. They better open this shit!"

The niggas had hos in the house, doing God knew what. I guessed that vaccine shot in the ass didn't stop the show.

We were locked out in the hot ass sun, smelling like the outside, and some hos interrupted what we had going on.

That didn't sit well with me and Tie. Trust me, we wanted to cut up, but we wouldn't do anything to damage Frank's mom's beautiful home.

My mind was a little foggy. We knocked again.

When they finally opened the door, my sister Tie punched one of the hos in her face. Bam! After Tie was done kicking her ass, all the hos ran off. Wanna and I hung out together. There were some dudes that lived in South Miami that me and Wanna knew. We used to catch the Metrorail to see them. We talked to them and had them come up to the Norland area to kick it with us.

Things didn't go the way we expected. We really thought we were going to hang out with them, be all up in the house you know, feeling jazzy while they whispered in a bitch's ear, but the fellas locked us out the door.

We were locked out again. They would not open the door. I guessed they were cock-blocking because my sister beat up one of their hoes they had up in the house, and they had us locked out in that hot ass sun.

When the dudes arrived, the driver accidentally hit the mailbox. We were laughing at them. The men in our crew were hating.

They did not let us in. The dude started doing donut spins in the middle of the road in a hooptie, talking shit because my bois wouldn't open the door.

Smoke erupted from the tires like smoke from a furnace. I thought his name was Keno. He had a twin brother.

To our surprise the fellas from South Miami still kicked it with me, Tie, Yaya and Wanna. Keno drove us to the 183rd Street Flee Market Parking Lot and we chilled. We enjoyed just talking.

Once Keno dropped us off at Frank's crib, my crew opened the door and let us in.

A few weeks later, we led the police on a high-speed chase. We were wild, and didn't know what to do with ourselves. When we were close to Opa-Locka, we jumped out of the car and started running. I mean we hauled ass to my great grandma Patsy's house.

We rushed inside and closed and locked the front door. My heart was racing. I really didn't know what to do. But I didn't panic.

Out of nowhere helicopters hovered above the house with spotlights on it. We knew the entire Opa-Locka Police Department. I didn't realize just how small Opa-Locka really was. Everybody knew everybody or was connected to somebody we knew.

Opa-Locka was all that I knew.

As for the Opa-Locka Police Department, the majority of them grew up with our parents; they knew each other, and their parents knew each other. Our older relatives knew the Commissioner and the Mayor. Our families were well connected in Opa-Locka, just to give an idea of how small it was.

So, for us to get arrested, we really had to do something bad, like something they had no choice but to put handcuffs on us. Because they did know our parents, our great grandparents, and our families.

It had to take an act of something big for them to arrest us, and even then, they would sometimes turn the other cheek and let us go home, or they just let us get away without saying anything.

Even though we got away from flying helicopters, even though we ducked police in pursuit of us, Detective Bowlegs still showed up on my great-grandmother's front porch and knocked on the door.

We didn't say shit. Detective Bowlegs walked to the side of the house and knocked on the side window. "Miss McCray, open the door. I need to speak to you. We know what y'all just did."

He must have thought I was stupid or something. All we did was shake and dodge cops when we were out hustling.

I said, "I'm not opening the door. If you don't have a warrant, if you don't have probable cause, if you don't have proof, and if you don't have evidence, this door stays closed and locked, Detective Bowlegs, no offense."

"Is that right?" He spoke. "You know, Miss McCray, if I wanna get you out of the house, you know I can get you out of the house, right?"

He wasn't backing down, neither was I.

I looked at him in the face through the window. "Well Bowlegs, you're gonna do what you have to do, and I'm gonna do what I gotta do. But I'm not opening that door without a warrant And clearly you showed up empty handed."

The helicopter continued to circle my great-grandma's house, shining that bright ass beam on us, casting shadows for the nosey folk that watched from the sidelines.

Detective Bowlegs squealed with joy. He thought it was funny. He stood there and laughed.

I didn't see what was so funny because initially I wasn't laughing at all, but my heart was pounding out of my chest.

Then, I started laughing, especially looking at the Detective get a kick out of this ordeal. Laughing actually caused me to calm down and keep myself together.

Shit, I'd been through and survived much harsher things than a laughing bowlegged Detective failing to get my young ass out of my great-grandma's house.

"Man, you know you ain't taking us to jail."

And he didn't. I honestly couldn't say if he decided not to take us to jail because he knew my great- grandmother, my mom, my dad, or my relatives. He just genuinely didn't take us to jail. Maybe he didn't have proof or evidence that we led them on a high-speed chase.

Only Detective Bowlegs could answer that question...

CHAPTER TWENTY-FIVE
THE SECOND RAPIST

I was 16 years old when I saw him, the monster that raped me, for the first time since it happened. I was with my sister Tie at The Liberty Market, located on NW 79th Street, in Liberty City. I took me and my sister shopping because, of course, I had come up on some money.

He started following us. He said, "Your face looks familiar...your face looks familiar."

I knew who the fuck he was. "Don't say nothing to him," I told Tie. "Don't say nothing to him."

"Who that is?" Tie asked me.

"Don't say nothing to him," I said, and I meant it.

When we entered a shop to buy items that we wanted, he walked in and said, "I knew I remembered you."

I snapped on his ass. "I remember you, too and I'm not a little fucking girl anymore. You better leave me the fuck alone if you know what's good for you!

I had a knife on me. I was going to stab his ass. He walked off.

"He raped me when I was younger," I told my sister, who was the first person I ever told. "If you ever see his face, you go the other way. And if he ever try to do anything to you don't be like me. You better scream and tell somebody."

That's what made me say something.

Chapter Twenty-Six: My Pa-Pa

Being 16, I was going to adult clubs. I was already living the fast life. It started for me when I was younger, dating big bois that had a lot of money. I was already a teenage mother, coming up with a teenage baby daddy, Fat Boi. My Pa-Pa forced me to get a job, and he was taking me to work.

He did that once before, when I was fourteen years old. He had taken me to the Jessica Center in Liberty City to get a summer job. He signed me up and took me to work for the whole summer.

He was preparing me for the future. He taught me how to earn my money, work for my money.

"Don't let a man stay home laying on his butt while you were cleaning, cooking, and taking care of the kids" he said sternly. "A real man did the opposite. He work and take care of his family."

That was how my Pa-Pa lectured me.

Honestly, I didn't listen to Pa-Pa, but as I got older, I took his advice. He planted the seeds that would one day sprout.

He would eventually tell me on his death bed, "You may not understand now, but soon I'll be dead and gone, but you're different, and you're special. And I want you to be there for your Mama (my great-grandma), and your siblings."

I promised him that I would. My daddy told me to keep my promises. If you felt that you would break a promise, just say that you'd try to do it. But if you promised, you better die and go to hell to make it happen.

I was 16 and cold-hearted. I already had a baby, I had been raped twice before I had a baby, my Mama used to abuse me for years, my brother used to beat on me as well because he was getting away with it. I had a lot of anger and resentment.

I regret the things I said to Pa-Pa when he was dying. I was old enough to know better.

He had one of his testicles surgically removed in hopes of saving his life, but he died anyway.

I recalled him running my friends from in front of the house.

I was fast in the ass, and thought I was grown. I talked back to him.

I told him, "Fuck you, fuck you! I can't stand you! That's why you got one ball! You got one testicle." I showed out in front of my friends, and when I got the phone call that he died, it stuck with me. It was a slap in the face.

I love him, I love him, I love him! I was trying my best to make up for how I talked disrespectfully to him. I wished I could tell him that I was damaged, mentally.

He was supposed to protect me against Mama.
I was so fucking damaged. I was so angry. I was so
resentful. I didn't know if I was worth it. I was
deeply hurt because I felt like my great-
grandparents could have helped me more against
Mama.

My great grandparents were old fashioned,
since the slavery days.

They were taught to turn the other cheek for a
lot of shit. And I felt like they could have protected
me against Mama.

I started doing cocaine.

I used to lace my cigarette with it, I put it in
my weed, and I took a one-on-one with a key or a
match. My younger sister had introduced me to a
dude she was messing with as a teenager that
became her second baby daddy. His name was
Nard. She was also a teenage mom.

I didn't like her dude at first. He was
outspoken, rude, and disrespectful. He was the one
that had me try cocaine, and he was seventeen.

Around that time, we were robbing old people,
but I gravitated towards hanging out with my older
cousin, Keyda. I was always under her, but I didn't
get to the point of being around her like I wanted
to because of the things I was doing when I was
leaving with men.

Some of the things I liked, and some of the
things I didn't. A lot of people I dealt with were
stabbing each other in the back. I knew a lot of
their secrets.

They had no idea what I knew, and I would
never put it in my book.

CHAPTER TWENTY-SEVEN
LEARNING MY LESSON

A lot of my older cousins were fucking with each other's main boyfriends and baby daddies, and I didn't like that shit, or the dishonesty.

There was no loyalty.

Then this cousin wanted to hang with this crowd, and the other cousin wanted to be around another crowd, and they started fighting each other.

I found another way to get money, I was still unemployed, so I started taking the shit I wanted. The only two jobs I had were the ones my Pa-Pa took me to.

My baby daddy was a few years older than me, and was heavy in the dope game. Big Ike was his daddy, God rest his soul. Street life was all my baby daddy knew.

My street mentality caused me to go after the men with the biggest dollar. So, my goal was to date a man that had something worth my time. I

rarely dated a man that was broke or had nothing
to offer.

It was easy for my fine ass to get money out of
Sugar daddies. I was pretty, light-skinned with
Chinese eyes, thick thighs, big booty, and a small
waistline. And I was clean, disease free.

The dudes I talked to weren't total strangers.
After we exchanged numbers, we got to know each
other over the phone.

I didn't just wham, bam thank you ma'am
with them. I didn't grow up with any of them, we
didn't know the same people, and we didn't have
mutual friends.

I knew their government names, where they
resided, if they were married or single, what kind
of cars they drove before I left with any of them. I
was smart, and knew how to protect myself just in
case things went south.

When my older cousins sent dudes my way,
they were men that they knew, personally, and
those men had something to offer.

I never met a dude and left with him right out
the gate. I wasn't that girl. I never walked the block
or stood on the corner with my ass out and my tits
sitting. I was too sadity and I had too much pride.

I frequented Miami Knights that turned into
Studio 183, in Carol City. It was located in the old
Plaza on NW 183rd Street and 27th Avenue where
the Flee Market used to be at. All the Ballers knew
it. When I stepped out in the streets, I looked and
smelled good.

I turned heads. I carried myself with class, like a lady. I dressed like I was in my mid-twenties, on my grown woman shit, getting the inspiration from Keyda. I would have hair down my back, or I rocked the short, feather cut. I had a banging body.

My four inch heels, miniskirts, and leather pants was emphasized by accessories and jewelry.

I wore the big dangly earrings, the real ones that cost over hundreds of dollars.

I was getting a lot of money out in the streets, hustling. Since I was younger than my much older, experienced cousin, Keyda, she introduced me to men who had a lot of money. I was raised on stereotypes when it came to men.

I also attracted men that found me desirable. All of my cousins prostituted, doing shit for money. Most of them.

There were different forms of prostitution. I wasn't on the hoe stroll in fishnet pantyhose.

A lot of my friends and relatives didn't agree with my definition of prostitution. And a lot of bitches that did what I was doing probably wouldn't agree with me, either.

Ninety percent of the girls I knew in Opa-Locka, even the chicks I grew up with, had left the club with men that gave them money.

If you were at a friend or relative's house, and you leave with a dude that gave you money, and he fucked, yes, that was prostitution.

One girl I know was like, "Yea, that nigga got this pussy, but I got that money!"

I didn't care what any of them had to say, they prostituted. I called them high class prostitutes.

When you exchanged sex for cash, baby, that was selling ass, prostitution.

It didn't take you to walk down the main avenue or flag down a car or get online to sell pussy.

When you were in the club, and you were looking like a thousand dollars in name brand shit, and all that ass was sitting, niggas were going to get at you.

There was an older moneyed dude that used to go to my cousin, inquiring about me.

"Keyda, who is that fine red bone that be with you. I wanna holla at her."

Translation, he wanted to fuck me.

Keyda came up to me. "What's up, girl, ole boy over yonder got $400. Are you gonna go home with him after the club closes?"

I was like, "Yea."

While they held onto the money, I left with the dude and we did whatever, whatever. The next day I got the money from my cousin and kept it moving.

Every two weeks, we were in the beauty salon getting our nails done. We were high maintenance females. That cost good money, you heard me.

I drank long island iced tea and a blue martini in the club. I used to drink straight liquor when I was younger, but I switched to Remy. No chaser, keep the rocks, pour it straight up, room temperature.

"Shanta" was my nickname since birth. When I turned fourteen, my cousins started calling me "China" because my eyes were slanted.

They were a group of women that were older than me. They went to elementary, junior, and McArthur North Senior high, an alternative school for bad students, together and remained tight.

The group of girls I met through my cousins, ironically, I met them in different areas, through different people. We all hung out together, in one big net of friends. Over the years, when I hung out, my great grandma Patsy helped raise my daughter.

She had the best clothes, jewelry, shoes, toys, food, you name it. I always got her hair done.

My great-grandma was a Christian, and old fashioned, set in her ways and her views.

When she kept my baby, there was certain places I wanted to take my daughter, but I couldn't.

Great-grandma told me, "No, you can't take her with you. The place is germy, and she needs to stay home."

I was on the fence, fifty-fifty, about it. On one hand, I didn't have any responsibilities. Great-grandma did everything, even baby sit.

I could come and go as I pleased, but on the other hand, I was like, "Damn, I can financially take care of my baby, and I don't have a say in her life?"

It was conflicting, but I reaped the benefits from it. When it came to prostitution, Rule number one, always get the money first. I recall hooking up with a dude I went to school with.

We were both damn near grown. I used to have a major crush on him, to be honest and transparent. I never told him. He was light-skinned with pretty eyes, just the way I liked 'em.

He propositioned me. "What's up, I have about $200."

"Is that right?"

"Yea...would you meet me at a motel, so we can, you know...I got you."

I was down. Business was business.

CHAPTER TWENTY-EIGHT
HIGH CLASS PROSTITUTION

Inconspicuously, we met up at the infamous Motel 6 on NW 27th Avenue and 135th. Everybody knew about this motel, and the freaky shit that went on behind closed doors.

I knew I was supposed to get the money, first, but I reneged on my own rules because I knew him personally from school and I had a crush on him at one point.

He was from Opa-Locka, he used to be on Ali Baba Ave.

Of course, it was a quickie.

He did use a condom. There was no foreplay, oral sex, nothing.

Don' get me wrong, the sex was good as fuck. He was packing, knew how to use it and all.

When we finished, we got dressed. We started smoking and joking around, enjoying each other.

After a short while, he stood up and said, "Hold up, let me go outside really quick. I'll be right back. I need to grab something."

I didn't think anything of it. I had a good quickie, I was getting $200, and I got to fuck the dude I always had a crush on in school.

Once he went outside, it took a while for him to come back inside. So, I went outside the door to check on him, buddy was gone.

He had cleared it like a stolen check. He left without paying me my money. Hit it and left.

I was pissed off, but I was embarrassed at the same time.

How could I retaliate or make a big scene about something that was illegal, something I wasn't supposed to be doing, and didn't want anyone to know that I did.

I chopped it up to the game.

Unfortunately, I saw him all the time after that, I just never spoke. I let it be.

Ironically, when he got out of jail after doing a stretch, he died in his sleep. I didn't know the reasons why, but I didn't feel any remorse. I wasn't saying that I was happy that he died, I just didn't feel anything once he did.

There was no love loss.

The second rule when it came to prostitution, and all of them broke this rule or didn't care about it, but I did (they taught me this rule), and this separated the hoes from the bitches.

You didn't fuck friends, and you didn't fuck relatives. By us being a group of girls, there would be one dude trying to talk to you and the girls (prostitutes) would fuck him, fuck the brother, then they would turn around and fuck the daddy, fuck the cousin for cash, and fuck your friends as well.

That gave the girls a bad reputation, and I wanted no part of that. I didn't break this rule.

No cousins or friends. That wasn't for me, and not the way I wanted to be remembered or did things. If you were in those streets, and you wanted to be respected, then there were certain things you couldn't do.

Dudes would slander your name when you fuck cousins, or you start loving the crew.

Then the rumors swirl, out of control, all over the 'hood, in every circle you were known if you broke the no friends and family rule.

"Aw, man, she's a ho," said one dude.

"Hell, yea, nigga. I had that bitch."

"I heard her own cousin paid for that pussy."

Thank God I was never slandered like that, all because I had class in everything that I did.

How could any of the girls get upset if dudes talked about them for breaking that rule?

Now don't get me wrong, I heard stories about a couple dudes I laid with, shit I never knew.

I hooked up with one dude, and down the line I hooked up with another one.

I could say that the worst thing to happen to me during this phase was not getting paid before laying with ole boi at the hotel.

I did like the benefits, which was the money.

The dudes that I hunched for money weren't dudes I just hunched all the time. I could call and be like, "Yo, I'm hungry," or "I need some money," or "I need my hair done," and they gave it to me.

I didn't have to hunch them for it.

I knew that once I reeled them in, once I had them in my clutches, I could get what I wanted without the hassle.

I milked them for what I could get. I burned my bridges, meaning that I begged and begged for cash until they got tired of me, changed their phone number, or cut me off all together.

Now I was trying to find myself. I was hurt, I resented myself, because I wasn't able to apologize to my Pa-Pa. I resented myself because I felt like I wasn't loved by my biological mother.

Truth be told, when I used to rob people, I loved it. It was a great rush, the adrenaline was high, and I was getting money. I didn't have to work, I didn't have to lay on my back and fuck for it, I just took other people's shit. It was my way of releasing my anger, and making money at the same time.

So, at age 16, Al gave us the idea to start robbing people.

My sister was pretty much the getaway driver. She never got out and robbed anybody. It was crazy. Her baby daddy went to jail when he was seventeen. He was sentenced to fifteen years in prison.

Another one of my brothers from another mother, Al, was sentenced to twelve years in prison, for crimes we did together.

Thank God for the no-snitching rule we had in place. Had they snitched, all of us would have done hard time together.

I was forever grateful that they didn't rat me out. I stuck by their side a lot of times when they were locked up in jail, but then they wound up getting hard prison time as teenagers.

I sent them money whenever I could.

I learned that I couldn't be tied to people I was cool with because people changed on you, and between us, things went south.

When I first started snorting cocaine, me, my sister's baby daddy at the time, and my friend Yaya, who was like my blood cousin, had driven off from my great-grandma's house and pulled up a few blocks back, and parked on the street Nathan B. Young Elementary was on, in Opa-Locka.

He had pulled out the cocaine and said, "Do you wanna try this?"

"No, I'm good," I said.

He was persistent. "Come on, try it!"

I gave him the side eye. "I...don't...know..."

"Try it!"

I tried it first. He talked me through it. He told me to snort a little bit once, then snort a little bit more. It went down my nose and my throat.

It was a rush, felt like a humble high. It wasn't like when you smoked it in a cigarette or with marijuana.

My friend Tiny then tried it, and ever since
that day we were snorting up a storm.

Chapter Twenty-Nine
Stripping

When I was little, me and my friend, who was more like a cousin, used to sit down and dream of being strippers. As little girls growing up in Opa-Locka, we used to be fascinated by the gorgeous strippers we saw leaving the Rolexxx, the most legendary strip club in the state of Florida.

They wore nice clothes, they rocked expensive jewelry, that had some expensive high heels, their makeup was flawless.

Those women were driving Lexus coupes, Jaguars, all types of luxury cars that I couldn't begin to name. The cars were always clean, sparkling, glistening under the moonlight as they slid up and down NW 27th Ave. to and from the Club.

That whole stripper life seemed like something ripped out of a page from a Hollywood movie. The glitz and the glamour, the beauty of the women, their curvaceous bodies that caused men to drool and cheat on their wives and give up their money, some of the fellas and big ballers gave these strippers their checks, income tax checks, child support money.

Niggas gave whatever for the booty, and we were hooked on what our eyes could see without understanding the dangers that lied behind the doors of a moneyed institution that saw strippers come and go.

The rumors ran rampant, the scandals out of that strip club was legendary and the secrets, private shows and prostitution only made the strip club more appealing.

Parking lot stayed on swollen status. Those strippers smelled, talked, and walked like they had money. And they did have money.

The hair was always laid and their bodies, oh my goodness, had horny men opening their wallets, buying them cars and condos, and dropped stacks on those women like money truly wasn't a thing.

That drew us to it, inevitably. The Big Bois, celebrities, or big ballers, used to come through and seemingly worship those strippers.

Ballers made it rain hundred-dollar bills before making it rain became a modern term in the culture.

I could remember the excitement in my friend's eyes as we talked about it. Oh, we're going to be like this, we're gonna be like that.

We're going to go out there and get that money. Going through that life gave the term you didn't know what you got into until you got into it a whole new meaning, especially when you could possibly get addicted to it.

I was 17 when I auditioned to be a stripper. By law you had to be 18 years old to be an adult exotic dancer, so I used my first cousin's ID and sped up the process a little bit since I was going to be 18 shortly after anyway. No harm in that right? Boy, was I wrong.

My cousin and I favored each other slightly, but not enough for me to slide on through her ID. That told me they really didn't care about my identity.

Not only was it a packed house, but those packed houses were also legendary by the time I started stripping.

I rushed into something I didn't quite understand. There was a lot of thoughts going through my head when I was going to my audition. The nice cars, the clothes, the money, the confidence that exuded from the strippers had me sold.

The way the men were willing to throw their life savings at them for just some form of attention was gold. I didn't realize attention came in many forms. And some of those forms I was not prepared for. I auditioned because I had to find a way to make money and take care of myself after my Pa-pa died.

For the audition I had to dance to three songs. This will be the real deal, the blood raw truth story of me becoming a stripper and what happened after I did.

At a club in Opa-locka, off of Northwest 27th Avenue right before NW 119th and the West View Apartments.

Club Lexusss. I promptly showed up, checked in, and gave them my ID.

I had on my outfit; I was holding my high heels. Three guys were in the room. One of them was the owner himself. I didn't know who the other two guys were. I think one of them was the DJ, as far as the other guy I have no clue who he was, and I didn't care.

I danced through one song with my clothes on. They watched and observed. Didn't do much of anything. A mixture of expressions. I wasn't focused on it because I was focused on doing what I needed to do to get to this money.

I danced to the second song with my top off. Having my breasts exposed, I didn't know how I felt, but for some reason I sort of felt empowered. Taking control of my life in some way, shape or form.

I was going after this money another way. I'd robbed people, I'd snatched purses and been in and out of the jail house. That life was not for me anymore. This was the start of the next chapter. And all that comes with it I must be willing to do, even if I didn't want to.

For the third song I danced naked. As I expected, I was hired. I was a bad bitch, 17 years old, using my cousin's ID posing like I was an adult. I felt like one, I was about to do grown woman things.

Most jobs you put in for you start the next week, but my start date was that night. Those niggas didn't waste no time.

No time to prepare, no time to wrap my mind around what I was about to do. We saw you naked, you auditioned, boom, now let's put your ass on the stage and see how much cash you could pull in.

That's basically what it was.

Honestly, I didn't like what I was doing from the start. But when you focus on making money, it didn't make sense if you don't take risks. When me and my friend were little girls dreaming about being strippers, we were blinded by the image, the cars and the clothes.

A life I wanted I instantly regretted after I started. This life was not for the faint-hearted, and it was not for everybody. This wasn't something as simple as dressing up and standing in front of a pole and turning in a circle. Oh no baby.

It was much deeper than that. For example, some of those strippers up in the club were having sex with each other in front of the Big Ballers in private areas. I was talking about all out sex.

The moaning, the oh's and the ah's, the bumping and grinding, the orgasms and shouts of pleasure, the titties flapping and the dominance all in the love of making money blew my mind.

Like it's just a thing to do within that belly and I was just getting started.

Some of the strippers left with moneyed men for money. Don't get it twisted, some of us had good sense. I wasn't the only stripper that rejected leaving the club with a man.

There used to be a man that came in there. He went back and forth to the bathroom, and I never knew why.

So, I asked the strippers, "Why is that man always in here for long hours at a time? Why is that man always running back and forth to the bathroom, like I'm confused?"

One of the strippers looked at me and said, "*Because* he has a rubber on his dick. He's constantly ejaculating. The rubber is so his come don't get in his clothes."

The man was her regular customer so that's how she knew what he was doing, and knew his personal information.

Strippers loved their customers. Customer satisfaction was number one. Baby, they go above and beyond for their customers.

Anything for that dollar they would do. If a customer happened to pull out a hundred dollar bill, those strippers we're going to do a little extra to get more.

They didn't stop, they kept going. Those bitches knew how to get money.

They took it seriously.

CHAPTER THIRTY:
STRIPPING, CONTINUED

They really felt like the customer was obligated and dedicated to only them. So, I'd be damned if you see another bitch walk up on one of her regulars.

There could be some potential problems.

Case in point, when the customer came to the strip club and he always asked for the same stripper, took care of the same stripper, dropped his money on the same stripper, if another stripper walked up on that man there was going to be problems.

Hos were slapping each other with chairs, bottles, and all. Do not step on another woman's toes up in the club.

Then there were the desperate women. They tried to force a lap dance on the customer when the customer really didn't want the lap dance. They were the worst. They gave all strippers a bad name.

Like damn, we were already stripping off our clothes, now you just going to force yourself on somebody who was just there for a good time, maybe a drink, maybe hung with the boys and enjoyed the view.

Window shopping. As long as he bought his drink minimum, he was good.

If a man came into a titty bar, you shouldn't have to go up to him and force yourself on him. Let him come to you naturally.

Just be yourself, do your thing, when you were on your A game a man was going to approach you anyway. But if you see he was not interested, or if he was interested in somebody else, let it stay at that. Just keep doing your thing, trust me, it's going to bring the big fish.

That's one of the reasons why men came to the strip club. To leave the nagging wives at home. The last thing they needed was a desperate woman and they just left one at home. That ruined the whole vibe.

Men liked options, so when they came in the club they were going to look around, buy them a drink, and take a pick from the cats in the litter box. That's the way it's always been. Once something captured his eye, he was going to approach you.

Of course, strippers come with different personalities. The different categories of strippers. Those that beg for dances. Those that leave the club and go tricking with a dude.

You have the thieving strippers that would steal your clothes the minute you turn your back. They go into your locker and took anything they could get their hands on and look in your face and make like they didn't steal shit.

Thieving hos that stole your money and your nigga. I was prepared by my cousin who worked at the club already. We were staying with our other cousin. She already assured me that she had my back, and she was a beast on that pole.

She told me to play with my hand close to my chest, make sure I always keep my money in my garter belt. Make sure your merchandise and your heels are properly locked inside your locker.

And do not leave your locker until you are sure it's secured. Me and my cousin shared the locker, so that eliminated any potential theft right there. Because my cousin was not the one to be messed with.

Me and her was in and out doing our set, so we took turns watching our locker until either of our sets were done.

We always kept an eye on our stuff. Hos was cutting the locks off the locker with bolt cutters if they saw you putting money in there, that's how desperate those women were.

This was the one that really got to me. Strippers would put drugs in your drink when you were not looking.

Roofies and pills, ecstasy, date rape drugs, stuff like that. Stuff that could potentially kill you or cause you some serious health problems just so they could get to your money.

Or get rid of you so they could take your regular customers. They smile in your face, but they were the main ones talking about you, causing problems for you, and trying to take what's yours.

You had the hos that would give you a lap dance and if you paid them a little extra, they'd ride that dick until it came, no questions asked.

I must admit that when the strippers participated in that kind of activity it made us look horrible. Especially to the strippers that were there to get through college, make extra cash for bills, not making it their whole life, or just there for the experience, to dance.

It made us all look like shit. Customers tried to force themselves on strippers as a result. Now customers wanted you to go home with them, begging and pleading for you to have sex with them, asking for fellatio, expecting us to be all out maids for the dick because of the bad apples in the bunch.

I wasn't with the program, nor would I ever be. There was one incident when a group of dudes came into the club to throw money around, throwing money in the air.

The strippers were over there eating. They were the envy of the other strippers that didn't get a piece of the pie.

A funny thing happened. When those that used to pursue me, or those that wanted to sleep with me found out that I was a stripper, they came to the club in droves looking for me.

That was the only time they saw me naked anyway. I didn't play that kind of stuff. I was offended at first. When people I knew was showing up just to see me naked. I didn't know how to take that.

Again, when you're on the outside looking in you didn't think about those kinds of things once you're inside. And now that it was happening, I didn't know how to feel. Should I be ashamed? Should I quit and get a day job? No, I focused on making that money. And I stayed focused.

Those I grew up with in Opa-locka, men that I would have never given the time of day, or even my conversation or something as simple as a glance, showed up at that club. I decided to look on the bright side.

At least they were people I knew, people I was familiar with, people I saw before. I was supposed to walk around naked anyway, so let's go make this money. At the end of the day, it's all about the money.

Word of mouth traveled fast around Opa-locka. The next thing I knew the word in the streets, the Nigga News, was "Oh, y'all heard Shanta stripping at the Club Lexx?"

Club Lexx was down the street from Club Rolexxx. The Rolexxx was the top dog of strip clubs, known worldwide.

There was no way my first time was going to be at the Rolexxx. Oh no, that was a monster I didn't think I could handle. They probably would have chewed me up and spit me out.

I was already making good money when the group of dudes walked in throwing money. So, while the strippers were dancing, shaking their asses, and having a gay old time, I was making my own cash, so I was good.

When the side show was over with, once the excitement died down and the cash stopped flowing, my cousin approached me with a proposition.

She said that the dudes wanted a few girls to take with them back to the hotel. I was looking at her because she was my cousin telling me this, and she should already know that I didn't leave with anybody.

I let her talk, to see exactly what the proposition was.

"You down, cousin?"

"Hell no. That's dangerous. You don't know what will happen."

"Are you sure?"

"Very. I'm good."

"Alright. We're about to leave. They're going to pay the bill."

"Pay the bill" meant that if a customer paid extra, the stripper could leave the club with him. You get charged for everything. You had to pay the DJ. If you decided not to get on stage, there was a fee. I knew that every establishment had rules and policies, but they were ridiculous with it.

In this case, since there was no real security to ensure that my cousin and the girls that went with the dudes to the hotel would be safe, guess what ended up happening.

My cousin came home, deeply upset, because it didn't go the way that she thought it would go. Making me happy that I stayed my butt away.

When they got to the hotel, the dudes robbed them of everything. Took it all. My cousin, her stage name was Lucky. She was a big weight in the stripping game. She took pride in her outfits. I was serious. Her costumes was custom made, all of that. One of a kind original piece.

I never saw those designs on any other female nowhere. They took the outfits, their money, and any possessions that they had. Left them with nothing.

Not only did the dudes take back the money they spent on the girls to get them to leave in the first place and to get them to do sexual favors, but they took the money that they made from the whole night.

Gone.

Even their jewelry. If their lace fronts wasn't sewn onto their heads, they would have taken them, too.

That was a lesson learned. I learned from the mistakes of my cousin and her stripper buddies.

I knew I wasn't leaving the club with strange dudes I didn't know.

Or anybody for that matter. I brought myself to the club, and I could take my own self home. With no problem.

Even though I was 17, I was very mature for my age. I had what they call an old soul. One of those souls that made you feel like you was here in a past life. I was more mature than a lot of the girls that I was stripping with.

I came on a whole different vibe, on a whole different level of getting money. I meant business, and I kept it business.

I kept my personal away from business. I was an experienced teenager. I was just different all together.

If I could go through what I'd been through leading up to that point, dealing with the police, robbing people and snatching purses, jacking people, dealing with brothers that shot at people, scoping out rich areas looking for people to jump out on, then I could deal with stripping.

I was trying to elevate in my life. Use that as a platform to come up in the world. I could have something to call my own. So, for me to be leaving the club tricking, no, that was a no-go.

I wasn't saying that the Price Is Right I just might like the rapper Trina in one of my favorite songs, but I thought about everything I did and at the end of the day I wound up not doing it.

CHAPTER THIRTY-ONE
QUESTIONABLE

I only stripped for a few months. And out of those few months I only showed up to do my set a few times. There really wasn't any money in it for me because my heart wasn't in it to start with.

It was just a dream of mine since I was a little girl that I fulfilled. That's where it started and stopped.

The most I made in one night was about $300, the bare minimum. That wasn't a lot of money if you thought about it.

Shaking my butt, my breasts all exposed, and not even break a thousand like some of the other girls?

I never stripped on the weekend. I really didn't want to strip when the club was packed to capacity, so I didn't. I didn't go to work every day. I did not strip 7 days a week. They were lucky they got me three days a week. I went in when I needed the money, it was not for the thrill of it.

One day I decided not to go to work. I didn't know why I had the desire to stay home, knowing I needed to go in to make money, but on my best night I only made $300 so I wasn't too excited about going in.

I stayed home. The very next day I went to work. As I entered the Club, some of the stripper girls rushed up to me.

I know they didn't miss me because I wasn't close to those thieving bitches like that, but something in my gut told me that I was not going to like what I was about to hear.

"Girl, you missed it!" Cream said excitedly, trembling all over.

"Gurl, missed what?" I asked. I really didn't care.

"Girl, your baby daddy was up in the club last night acting a fool! His wife or his girlfriend, whoever she was, was snapping, too."

I stifled a yawn. "No offense, but what has that got to do with me? I have things to do. I don't have time for rumors, and I don't worry about what my baby daddy is and is not doing. He got his life, and I got mine and you need to mind your business."

"It has everything to do with you because he was up in the club looking for you!"

My eyes bulged out of my head. "Are you serious? No, that muthafuckah wasn't looking for me," I said dismissively. "He left me for whoever she is that's acting crazy. Me and her have no association with each other and we are not friends."

"Chile, you could have fooled me. All I know is that he came through the front door, asking questions about you. Looking for you, searching for you. He wasn't going to leave until he found you.

"And didn't believe that you was not at work," she continued, getting a kick out of it. "He was convinced that you was hiding in the back and that we were protecting you or something. Which is why he started acting like a fool."

" I can't believe what I'm hearing."

"Girl, that's not it. His baby mama, his wife, his girlfriend or whoever she is, was outside the entrance doors, yelling. She was riled up. She said that she knows your baby daddy is inside the Club to see you, that word around town coined you as a stripper and everybody coming here to see you so why her baby daddy is up in there trying to see his baby mama behind her back. She acted a complete fool. Security rushed outside."

"Fuck."

"Security was telling her that your baby daddy was not inside the club. They denied that he was even in the building, but she didn't believe it at all. She was not leaving. And she was not happy. Girl, a crowd gathered outside the club. That's how angry this girl was that her baby daddy was potentially inside with you."

"This is crazy."

"She was trying to push her way inside. She did not see Security and snubbed them when they tried to restrain her. All she knows is that her man was inside the club doing something with you.

"And she wanted to get inside to find out. But security was not having it. They told her she could not come in the club, and they made sure she didn't come in the club. Meanwhile, your baby daddy snuck out the back exit while all this was going on."

A few days later we wound up talking and it wasn't pretty. He accused me of being an unfit mother because I was stripping.

He said that he was going to take my daughter from me through the courts.

He didn't want me anywhere around my child, that she would be better off with his doggish ass.

That was the joke of the century. Nigga, stop reaching. I wasn't trying to hear him. He did not intimidate me, and he was not going to take my daughter.

That was my child. I carried her for 10 months. I did everything for my child. I made sure my child ate. I did this to make sure my child continued to eat. That roof over her head is her security.

That means everything to me. And anything that stands in the way of that will see these hands.

"Whatever, I don't give a fuc~"

"Especially my baby daddy, a man that left me for the female that was outside the club trying to get inside it while you snuck out the back door. Where was this when your baby mama was trying to get through security to get to your dumb ass ? If you're a man, if you're a fit father, why didn't you go outside and confront her when she was in front of security. I would have respected it more, but you're getting all up in my face, but you didn't get all up in your ho's face. Boy goodbye, good night, the end."

Mind you I was seventeen years old. I gave birth to my daughter when I was thirteen. He didn't do a thing for his daughter. He was not there for her in any way, since she was two years old because he had got him a new girlfriend.

By this time his new bitch was either pregnant or she'd just given birth to his second child. His second child and our daughter was almost three years apart, so yea he and his whatever had that baby already, and he was worried about me and mine?

Chile, please. He didn't buy a box of diapers, he didn't send me money towards any daycare, he didn't come spend any time with her; he didn't come read bedtime stories to her.

He didn't come protect her from the boogie man under the bed, he didn't come put up a Christmas tree and buy her gifts and help me wrap them up.

He didn't teach her how to walk. If he had to answer the million dollar question, what was his daughter's first word, he would lose.

Was he eligible for Father of the Year? His greatest achievement was leaving me for the woman that swore he was up in the club with me.

So, your decision making was questionable.

I was still messing around with my baby daddy. I was naïve and foolish. I felt dumb, like why did I want to keep messing around with someone that didn't want all of me or his child.

He just wanted to take his pick, explore his options while I was raising our daughter.

He wasn't doing shit for me or his own flesh and blood.

In reality I only kept doing shit for him because he was my man first and that was a dangerous way to think, especially when he shitted on me for the next bitch.

A bitch that acted evil towards me, like I gave a damn. She didn't play fair, and she was nothing nice. I was like, "Ho, you think you got my man, but you don't…"

I refused to get sucked into her bullshit, especially over a bullshit man and an even shittier father.

She played for keeps. She didn't care, neither did I. Before she got pregnant, she was loving my daughter. She took her on trips and all, but when she gave birth to her baby, it was fuck my daughter. It was all about her baby.

You had to love yourself more than that, but I was grown and hardheaded.

My baby daddy wouldn't give me my daughter. He stayed in Clover Leaf. I wanted my baby, and I meant business.

I told him when I got there, and he didn't give me my daughter, there was going to be a problem.

"You're a mufucking stripper, you unfit

mother."

Ok. When I arrived, I was G.I. Jane. Bitch, I had a knife, a gun, roach spray and a lighter. Yea, roach spray and a lighter.

Out of all three of those options, I was going to light their asses up, him and his ho.

I didn't want to shoot or stab them.

I was going to be an arsonist and burn that apartment to the ground.

You didn't do shit for my baby, and you thought that you was just going to show up and take her from me?

Nigga, you got me all the way fucked up.

That nigga showed up with my baby, bet his ass he did. I was not fucking around. I was about to spray and light, ready to go to war.

I drove off with my daughter respectfully and I didn't have to act an ass, because if it's one thing you'll find out about me...

Shanta acted an ass and I'll put my foot in your ass if you come for me. And that was a wrap.

Moving on. Stripping through the week worked better for me, because people were either at work or in school.

The traffic through the club was slim to none and that gave me more time with my daughter.

The crowds came in after the sun went down on the horizon like freaks when they came out at night. 10:30 or 11:00, 12:00, going into 1:00 a.m.

Horny dudes with the money, those that want to be entertained, those that were quietly preying on us was the crowd.

You never knew what danger walked through the doors until you were in a situation you couldn't get out of.

That led to me turning my back on it.

That life was not for me.

It was a wrap.

Game over.

Looking back as that little girl that admired the strippers, that drove all the flashy cars and had even flashier jewelry, had all the dudes lusting after them, seemed like a dream.

But once I was in that dream, that life was not for me.

CHAPTER THIRTY-TWO: MYSTERY

I met a dude named Patrick Joseph, who was 7 years older than me. We met the day I was sitting on my great-grandma's porch, broke as fuck, looking for another hustle, another come up.

My way of a "come up" was simple. I'd look through my phone to see who I could call, who I could page.

That was one way I kept money, or I found out through the proper channels about the next scam or scheme, i.e., bank schemes, credit card fraud, etcetera. I was on it.

He was driving by my grandma house in a raggedy light green Nova, with a car full of dudes. He saw me, my sister and a couple girls on the porch, vibing and someone called out, "Hey!"

The car stopped in the middle of the road, then the driver backed up to us on the porch.

All of the dudes got out of the car at my great-grandma's house, trying to holla. Me and my girls checked them out.

My older cousin always gave me a checklist
when it came to finding a good dude.

There was an old school song called "B Girls,"
by Young and Restless, a rap group that summed it
up.

B stands for Bronco, Benz, BMW, Bass...

If you were from Dade County, you know the
"B Girls." song. I was going down the checklist,
consciously.

He didn't have a Bronco, Benz, BMW or a
Cadillac Brougham.

Ok, they were on the Avenue like they were
stars.

The driver had eyes for me. He approached
me. "Hello, how are you?"

I smiled. "I'm good."

"What's your name, and how old are you?"

"My name's China, and I'm seventeen."

I looked him over. Even though he didn't fit
the "B girls" criteria, he did have pretty eyes, he
was very handsome, and he was well dressed in
expensive clothes. I had expensive clothes as well,
so I could spot flee market shit in a heartbeat. I
was stealing clothes from all the department stores,
like JCPenney, Macy's and Burdine's, so I knew
the details in authentic designer clothes.

I was raised to look a man from the feet, up.
And he looked good. His car was raggedy. He
wasn't wearing big chunks of jewelry.

Despite the age difference, I still talked to him
anyway...

CHAPTER THIRTY-THREE: MONSTER

I was eighteen when I saw him again, the dude that abducted me and raped me in Liberty City. Only this time I found out who he was. Keyda had a friend named Big Titty Robin that hung out at her house in the Poke-n-Bean Projects, of 13th Place and NW 63rd. That was my cousin's first government housing unit.

That monster was Big Titty Robin's fucking boyfriend. When I saw his face, I took a deep breath. That was the first time I told my cousin what that monster did to me, and the second person I told since my sister Tie at the Liberty Market.

Keyda didn't believe me. She was like, "What?"

Apparently, he was a very well-known, popular dude that girls liked. I found out his name was Keith.

I told Keyda, "Yes, he raped me, cousin."

I gave her the whole rundown. She said, "Are you sure its him?"

"I'm telling you that's him, cousin. I'll never forget his face."

The bitch didn't believe me. Yes, she was a bitch because I know she second guessed me after I told her I was raped.

She was a bitch from that point on. Why wouldn't she believe me? His name was Keith, and his girlfriend was Big Titty Robin.

CHAPTER THIRTY-FOUR
ABORTION

I was 18 years old when I was pregnant for the second time, with my second child. My sister, who was 16 years old, who had just had a baby I was also taking care of, was also pregnant with her second child.

At this time, Markeisha was going on five years old. I had just met a good man that had a lot of money. He was taking care of me, taking care of my family.

Even though my great-grandma told me I wasn't going to have any more kids, this turned out to be prophesy.

I couldn't keep the baby. It wasn't Patrick's.

Well, I made a choice not to keep the baby.

Was it to keep a relationship with him because he had money and was taking care of me and mine? Or was it something else? Was I being selfish? I had just met him.

Did he know that I was pregnant? No. I kept it to myself. Everything wasn't for everybody to know.

That was the fastest way to chase away a new man in your life. Tell him that you were pregnant.

I actually had Patrick take me to the doctor's office. While I was seeing the doctor, he stayed out in the Waiting Room. Once I was done, I walked up to him. "I had a stomach virus," I lied.

That same week, I had Patrick take me to my great-grandma's house.

"I'm going to stay here with my daughter for a few days."

"You're going to be good?"

"Yes, I will."

Let me rewind a little bit. Me and Tronie was messing around for a couple of months. I had a one night stand with Chucky, while I was with Tronie. I met Patrick afterwards, when I was sitting on my great-grandma's front porch. I dumped Tronie for Patrick. Tronie was my age, and Patrick was 27-years old. Once Patrick left, I had Tronie, who I tricked into thinking he was the real father, take me to get an abortion.

My great-grandma knew that I was pregnant because I was really sick for two or three months before I found out I was pregnant.

Once I got back from killing my baby, she knew that I wasn't pregnant anymore. She started praying every time that she saw me.

Praying, and praying and praying.

Because I knew better. Really.

I was empty inside. No matter how many times I tried, I couldn't get pregnant after that. I could never have any more kids.

I was deeply hurt. I sacrificed and raised other people's kids. I couldn't count two or three of those kids that I raised that would even acknowledge me. And I killed my unborn child for them. I felt like a murderer. The older women, they were six, seven years older than me, were having three, four and five abortions at a time, like it was nothing.

I only had one, and I could never have any more. I instantly regretted it, and I couldn't take it back or make it go away. I made a vow that one day I was going to tell young women my story. It was not cool to kill babies or have an abortion.

You could change your mind, but you couldn't go back once you go through with it. There were no do-overs. No one understood how badly I wanted to go back and stop myself from taking the life of my second child. Markeisha would have had a brother or a sister. I robbed my daughter of a sibling. For what? A man with money?

I was getting into scamming. I started opening lines of credit and paying off **the balance** from Burdine's, Macy's and JCPenny. Burdine's was my first credit card. Chile you couldn't tell me I wasn't doing it. The old heads remember the nineties, if you were going to get a credit card Burdine's was the sure shot and the hot trend down south.

They'd easily approve you for a hundred, two hundred dollars; a credit limit that was easy to pay down or pay off, and that gave you clout to get approved for other credit cards.

Chicks walked around like they were fancy with the Burdine's card.

You'd swear they were celebrities, on the local level. Burdine's was a popular place that branched off into other stores.

I had Burdine's, then Macy's, then my JCPenny cards, and in that order.

My own Mama used to wear my expensive stuff to the crack house. She used to steal my expensive clothes that I stole from Burdines, Macy's and other department stores.

She was the cleanest bitch in the crack house. You had her fucked up! She was styling and profiling in my stolen shit. She'd even wear my panties. I stole clothes with Kena. We started stealing together as teenagers. She was my baby daddy's family.

I was in a relationship with a Haitian dude I met back when I was 17 going on 18.

I was like, damn, I need some type of hustle that didn't involve purse snatching or robbing people.

I wondered what was going to be my next come up, and when because shit was real out in these streets.

CHAPTER THIRTY-FIVE
THE MONEY

I lived with my moneyed Haitian boyfriend, Patrick Joseph. He took care of me for two years, like I was a queen. I moved out of my great-grandma's house to be with him. My daughter lived with my great-grandma Patsy. He had everything a man with money could ask for.

Instead of building me up and encouraging his woman to live out her own aspirations and dreams, he unapologetically hindered me.

Before I met him, I was on the scene making my own bread, my own moves, keeping a bitch out of my face. I didn't need a nigga or my sorry baby daddy for shit. After we met, his ol' jealous ass was against female empowerment.

He moved me to Fort Lauderdale and pretty much threw me in a room and the rest was history.

The location and the neighborhood was nice. We lived in an efficiency on the side of the house. It had its own room, walk in closet, spacious bathroom, a king sized bed fit in there as well.

There was also an adjoining door that led to the main house. His mom and brother lived on the other side of that door.

Don't get me wrong, we went out sometimes, but if I wanted to go out by myself, he'd rent me a car so I could drive back to Opa Locka, or he'd drive me, to see my family and friends or go shopping, but I had to tell him where I was going and what time I was coming back.

I was on a time frame to make it back to Fort Lauderdale from Opa-Locka, like I was on a curfew.

If he wasn't with me, he'd stay on the phone with me the whole time like cyber security, wanting to know my every move. What in the Bell South kind of shit was that?

After being with him for a year, he took me to another house in North Lauderdale. It was a beautiful house.

Everything was white with no hint of black. House rule, I had to take my shoes off at the door.

It had a jacuzzi, expensive trinkets, you name it.

We wound up staying in what I suspected was one of the guest rooms because, with a house this beautiful there was no way this simple-ass room was the Master bedroom.

I found that quite odd, but I put it out of my mind.

I thought to myself. I had a lot of questions. We never stayed overnight in somebody else's house. We always lived in an efficiency at his Mama's house.

Why now?

I looked at him. "Who's house you brought us to?" I asked, curious and yes, I needed an answer.

This nigga said, "My house" without batting an eyelash.

I was confused. If this was his house, why were we living at his Mama's house, even though it was an efficiency, it was still attached to the side of the side of Mama's house.

"Your house?"

"Yes, baby."

"With your name on it, you paid for it?"

"Yes, I own this house. I lived here with my ex-fiancé at one point, but I never sold or got rid of the house."

"Okay."

I guess my facial expression gave away how I felt. I sat there looking crazy or like a fool, take your pick. I was in a relationship with a big-time drug dealer.

When we met, he drove an unflattering antique car with a funny shape, odd color and a hard top. He was being inconspicuous, I guessed.

I never knew and he didn't tell me that he was slinging dope in the 'Hood. The car threw me off and probably the Feds, too. So, I never thought to ask him what he did for a living, his profession.

Then we gradually got to know each other.

He was always taking me out on dates, showing me a great time, but what threw me was how nice the car was.

It wasn't the out-of-space antique hardtop.

The new car was bad ass, complete with gold rims, stereo system, and all.

"Baby, who's car is this?"

"It's my car, baby."

"Ok."

I also noticed how iced out he was with chunks of diamonds. I was quiet. He wore mediocre clothes when we first hooked up.

I still went with him because he was handsome, and I loved his brown eyes. I was branching out on my own.

I started making my own decisions when it came to me and my daughter's well-being.

I was tired of running behind older chicks trying to do what they do, but never worked out for me in the end.

A lot of heartbreak, betrayal and tears came from older chicks thinking for me.

Now my mediocre boyfriend looked like he stepped out of *New Jack City*, Haitian style when we went on dates.

He had more money than you could shake a stick at, and I had no clue.

Chapter Thirty-Six
My first real Relationship

Cars started dropping out of the sky because he had so many. He was the Boss and in charge of a whole entourage of niggas, sending my suspicious mind into overdrive.

Rum and Pub used to be jumping back in the day. I was there with my cousin and my clique.

My jealous boyfriend came, and I knew how he was.

He drove a bad ass car on gold rims. About ten of his bois were in their pricey cars, all on gold rims behind him.

The music from all twelve cars thumped, shutting the whole block down.

He drove up next to me and his bois all backed up and parked while he looked up at me with a smile and those brown eyes.

"What's up, baby?"

My clique stared in awe with their mouths dropped open, wide eyed, like it was raining dollar signs. All twelve cars were glistening under the streetlights.

Moneyed Zoes were chunked out with diamonds. Jewelry is worth more than a damn house.

They came from North Lauderdale and shut that shit down at the Rum and Pub Club in Carol City. All eyes were on them.

My girls were lit with space and opportunity.

"Damn, China. You are doing it like that, girl?"

I felt like I was the only girl in the world in his eyes. My girls gave us some privacy by walking over to the other cars in the entourage and started flirting with the Zoes.

My boyfriend and I were laughing.

He loved every moment of it.

His Haitian ass loved the fuck out of me, and I loved the fuck out of him. Our relationship was strained at times.

He took a young girl from the streets, put me in a room at his Mama's house and loved me up, but never pushed me to be something great in my own right, outside of him.

He figured that I didn't want anything out of life. As the older person, he could have built me up to bring the best out of me with the same energy we fucked, but it was not to be.

That was all I was to him.

A walking trophy.

He kept me locked in the house, gave me money, took me shopping at the best stores, bought me expensive jewelry, buttered my cakes, but never cared about my interests.

I didn't think he ever asked me what I wanted to do with my life. I didn't even ask myself.

He could have said, "Bae, if you enroll in a school to learn a trade or be a nurse, I'll take you."

But when love was not on the brain what else was there to look forward to.

I was submissive, doing whatever he wanted, running behind him. Some women wanted a Made Man.

Someone who had his shit together and had his own, thinking he'd just fall in their lap. It didn't work that way with me.

If a man had it together and his woman didn't, but she had potential, why not give her a chance, and encourage her to be better if he liked or loved her.

Pull her under his wing.

Those made the best relationships, building and growing together.

You didn't always meet your equal, someone on your level, at hello and a handshake. Sometimes you had to make your equal.

Unfortunately, that didn't matter when all he gave was material possessions and a good nut.

I guessed our relationship was a wine and dine affair.

There for a good time, not a long time.

I said that because, out of the blue a woman started calling and harassing us.

"Who is she?"

"Nobody."

One day in North Lauderdale I was in front of the house talking to my boyfriend. In a zone, we were enjoying each other's company.

We were caught off guard by a bitch that pulled up on us, talking shit. She was bold and didn't give a damn, nor did we.

For the life in me I had no idea who she was, but I was on guard, and I'd clothesline the bitch if she got out of pocket.

I was with my boyfriend for over a year, and out of blue, boom, another ho. Before I could do anything, my sister Tie sprayed mace in her face.

She disabled her ass at hello. We were 'bout that life and the life after that life in these parts.

After all the shit she talked, that mace in her eyes had her running, screaming in agony. Once she got to her car she jumped in, and she pulled off.

I figured that was the chick that kept calling and harassing us, had to be. I would remember her face and that bat mobile she pulled up on us in.

I said bat mobile because she thought she was a superhero and mace turned her ass away, pronto. You didn't just pull up on a bitch.

Luckily no one had to pull the strap.

As the days progressed, yes, she was a hood rat, fleabag ho my man was fucking around with in the Projects before I came on the scene.

He clearly moved on, but she couldn't take that he fell in love with me, and she became a distant memory.

Some women hate rejection. She had her chance to win him over. He was telling her crazy ass that he was over her, that he moved on, as a real man should, but she didn't take "no" for an answer. I must admit that she was consistent, but that consistency would make me kick her ass and I had a daughter to raise.

"You want this, you can't get over this. She can't treat you like I did, nigga! You'll come sniffing around again!"

She wasn't a threat. All bark and no bite. I put it out of mind and continued living my life, doing my thing as his submissive girlfriend.

Before I knew it, we were approaching our two year anniversary. I didn't remember what holiday was coming, for the life of me I was trying to remember, but I was chilling in the room at his mom's house when the phone rang.

There was a direct private line in our room, so I didn't have to go into the big house to take a call or make a call. I could just make one in the privacy of our efficiency.

We didn't give out a number unless it was somebody we really knew, or established a relationship with.

I answered the phone after a few rings. Just because it rang didn't mean I broke my neck to see what somebody wanted.

People only called when they wanted or needed something and once they got it, you never heard from them until they needed something else.

"Hello," I began, politely.

"Hello, may I speak to Pat?"

"He's not here..."

"May I ask who I'm speaking to?" she asked.

"You called him. I'm his girlfriend, now who are you?"

"This is his ex-fiancé."

I idled down. I wasn't upset or suspicious. I already knew he had an ex-fiancé; I just never met her or spoke to her until the phone call.

"Okay, but what do you want with me?"

"I'm going to be honest with you, woman to woman. Completely transparent so there is no misunderstanding or confusion. Pat really does love you, and I love the man I'm in a relationship with. Pat and I never made it to the I Do's because we kept bumping heads, and it didn't work out. We came close to exchanging rings before two families, but now we want to give it another try."

I hopped up to my feet, heated, but I kept it together. "Hold up, hold up. What do you mean that y'all are going to give it another try?"

"I'll tell you exactly what I mean. Pat and I are together. You and Pat are over, through, done with. Fortunately, for me, and unfortunately for you, Pat and I started talking again behind your back."

"Bitch, what are you talking about?" My nerves were boiling. I could barely breathe.

"Remember when he sent you back home to Opa-Locka for two weeks?"

I said, "Yea, but how do you know about it?"

"He sent you back home because he rented a Winnebago—"

What the hell was a Winnebago?

"—And me, Pat, his two friends, my sister, and my cousin took a road trip to Disney World."

"What...?" Was she serious? Behind my back while I was at home as his unsuspecting, submissive girlfriend? And he took a step back?

"True story."

"You mean to tell me that he had me pack up most of my stuff after being stuck in a room at his Mama's house for two years, drove me to my great grandma's house and said he would be back and the whole time I'm with my family, you and him are rekindling your relationship. Did y'all go down memory lane remembering the good times that inevitably led y'all back together? And y'all went on a road trip in a house of wheels?"

"Yes. Pat and I are getting back together. I am truly sorry for having to tell you this or even having to say this, especially this way. I'm not intentionally trying to hurt your feelings, but the heart wants what the heart wants. Truly, you underst—"

I hung up in her face. I started cleaning up our spot. I paused when I saw a lighter that was as long as my middle finger.

The design on it read "Welcome to the World of Disney."

My heart dropped into my stomach the same time the lighter slipped from my lifeless fingers and fell on the floor. Confirmation.

"What the fuck have you done, Pat?"

I broke down into tears, so weak in the knees I could barely stand. With trembling hands, I called Tammy, one of my friends who was like a big sister and tearfully told her what happened.

She came over in a heartbeat from Scott Projects. I didn't pack all of my shit. I packed what I could and hauled ass.

His Mama must have heard me leaving. No, there was a camera I didn't know about. As I was leaving out the side door she came out of the front door, intercepting me.

"Where are you going?"

I didn't see her ass. "I'm leaving, that's where I'm going. I am done!"

"Patrick no say you can leave! Come back here! Patrick no say you can leave!"

I hopped in Tammy's car and hauled ass. Left her in a cloud of smoke. I was a grown woman with a baby. I came and went as I damn well pleased. Not only was I crushed and devastated, but he also didn't fight for me anyway.

At least I knew why we stayed in the guest room at that nice house in Fort Lauderdale, he once lived in with his ex-fiancé. He purposely didn't take me to the Master Bedroom because he kept that shit sacred for that bitch.

I was such a lovesick fool. He wanted her back. I was baffled. I was with him for two years.

After all we'd been through together, he abandoned me and had another bitch call the land line to do his dirty work because he wasn't man enough to do it himself.

We never had an argument or a fight. I did everything I was told. The few times we did mess around after I moved out, he treated me like I was nobody, like I was just another ho from the street.

This was the man that was buying my jewelry, my clothes, getting my hair done, nails and feet done, rented me cars, wined, dined, and made me and he now looked at me like we were strangers meeting for a booty call or a one-night stand.

He was the one loving me, kissing me, hugging, and protecting me. He said that he was a real man. And I believed it until I found that Disney World lighter.

He once treated me like a Queen. Now he just wanted to fuck me. My foolish ass still hooked up with him once after that.

We stayed the night in an expensive hotel. Not once did he ask was I hungry, how my day went, nothing.

After we fucked, he drove me back home in silence. I was destroyed. Once I got out of the car and he drove off, I cried like a baby.

I was deeply hurt.

He claimed that it was my fault that he moved on because I shouldn't have left that room at his Mama's house. I should have stayed. By me leaving he made up his mind on what he wanted to do.

He flipped the shit on me. How in the hell. He had his nerve. I was supposed to stay there until he made up his mind? I wasn't with the fuckery. He was saying in so many words that my leaving forced him to go back to her.

Once I got back to Opa-Locka, I moved back
into my great grandma's house. I didn't want to go
back there, but I had no choice.

I didn't stay with her for long, maybe a week
and some change.

CHAPTER THIRTY-SEVEN
EXHAUSTED

My first cousin's first cousin offered me a room at her place if we split the bills down the middle. She lived in the Yaway buildings in Little Haiti, on NW 62nd Avenue. I took her up on the offer. I was like, "Alright."

I made that move quick, fast and in a hurry. We lived together for about a year. By that time, I'd gained weight and it wasn't cute. I used to be fine. I couldn't have that, so I started power walking every day until I lost that weight.

We moved into a bigger place down the street because it was me, my baby, her and her boyfriend. After letting a nigga take care of me for two years hindered me because when he left me for his ex-fiancé, I didn't have a job, I wasn't in school and with a daughter that was a no go now that I lived with somebody, splitting the bills.

It didn't take me long to find a new hustle that didn't involve purse snatching or robbing people. I was over that life.

I was back hustling in the streets. After a while I got into scams. It didn't involve a gun or running up and down the block with a stolen purse under my arm like I was running cross country track in high-school, sweating out my hairstyles and shit.

I grew accustomed to a good lifestyle, so I wasn't going to take a step backwards and live like a broke bitch. I knew my worth, and I got out there and made it happen.

I wasn't going to sweat niggas, kiss a nigga's ass or be a wife to niggas when I was just a girlfriend. I learned how to be submissive to me, myself, and I.

I wasn't bending over backwards for niggas because they gave me money and jewelry and expensive name brand clothes and when I get stuck on a nigga, he promise me the world just to fuck me when and how he wanted and still left me for the next bitch or a bitch he was already fucking around with.

Leaving me with nothing but heartbreak and hurt. I took it to the next level. I started scamming, big time. I was going on nineteen years old.

I didn't qualify for welfare. The main office felt that with the rent and utilities I was splitting with someone in a two-bedroom apartment in Little Haiti proceeded the income bracket with one child.

However, I was approved for food stamps and Medicaid, but I wasn't approved for a welfare check.

Needing a quick come up, I contacted a couple dudes from my past that I was still cool with, and I knew they still liked me, and they paid some bills.

So that was one way, but not good enough.

Then I got into income tax scams. I got ahold of a dude that was located by 441 and 200th Something Street. My job was to find people who didn't work and get them the file their taxes. He would get a portion and I would get a portion. I would do this for a few years.

I wouldn't say the name of the business, and I wouldn't say his name, but on 200th Something Street the business grew from a small office to an upstairs building with him owning nearly the entire floor. I made him a lot of money.

I wasn't saying that I was the reason he got a bigger office, but partially I was. I didn't know where he was getting those W2's o, but he was getting those non-working people that money and taking our cut off the top.

I didn't know about him, but down the line I had to pay the IRS that money back. I found out what he was doing and how he was doing it.

He was filing W2 forms from companies that was closed down, out of business. When it was time for me to be audited ten years later, I had no proof for those W2 forms. The government had a copy, and it was up to me to keep up with my copies, and I hadn't.

I went back to the tax file, but the proof wasn't there. Therefore, since I received the money, I had to pay every last dime to the penny back.

I'm going to rewind this tape for a minute. I'll get back to that.

Like I said, it was my job to recruit people. But one thing about me was I was an honest criminal. If you were a friend, family, or someone that was referred to me, or working with somebody that was referred to somebody connected to me, I always gave them anywhere from $200 to $350 for each person they found for me because I was eating.

Boss man was already getting them $8,000 to $10,000 back. He takes about $4,000 for himself. The recipient was getting a few thousand and I was getting $2,000 a pop.

And then I started getting double the money when I started flipping my client's kids that had socials for a fee.

Someone would be like, "I know somebody that wants to buy some kid socials."

And I'd be like, "I know someone with them for sale, but you gotta give me the money." That's what I mean by flipping kid socials.

People that didn't work filed only two of their kids and had three more they didn't file, but sold those three socials to someone looking to add kids to their W2's for a bigger payday.

For someone that was unemployed with no kids I'd add one of more of the unused kid socials from my clients and it all balanced out.

I was flipping that shit. Eating, baby, I was eating!

So, when I moved down South, I was still doing the income tax shit, but business was slow.

Not only did it slow down, it came to a halt because of my conniving sister Tie, with her fuck ass.

What happened was that when the income tax things started to slow down or did slow down, she found somebody, like I had, and she needed some customers.

I told her ok and I sent the customers to her. At the same time, I had other people outside of her that still wanted to sell their kid's information for profit, but they didn't want to file because their files were already known.

I sent my customers to Tie and she fucked everybody. Not only did she not give the clients their money, but she recycled their information for years. Tie had clients tied up in the system for years as well.

She had me looking stupid. And by doing that she took bread out of my pockets. My reputation was shot because of the backhanded things that she did. I'm gonna do a whole segment on my sister Tie because people need to know exactly what she did.

Yeah, I could talk for hours about her ass.

Not only that, but she has also done things to me for a long time, things that I was going to get into because she was my own flesh and blood, and she would do me this way.

She didn't deny her wrongdoing.

I was now living in Little Haiti. I was about to turn twenty years old. My great-grandma's house made headlines when it was burned up in 1998. It was gutted. She didn't have insurance, so she suffered a huge loss.

They were living pillow to pole in a hotel on Biscayne for about a month. It was heartbreaking and tough. Emotions ran high. The American Red Cross funded the stay through a voucher.

Unfortunately, the money ran out from the voucher, so they could no longer stay in the hotel. I went and spoke to the landlord of the apartments I resided in Little Haiti.

Great-grandma was able to move into a place at last minute notice.

The American Red Cross and a second agency helped them move in and the agency gave the landlord a check to cover the costs.

The apartment was the only place I could find to get my family moved in fast.

Now, my family living in Little Haiti where I was located. And through them I was informed about a resourceful lady that lived upstairs who knew somebody that could get $10,000.

That piqued my interest because, at this point, my hustle with the tax man faded to black. It was completely over. Shut down. Tie had burned, betrayed, and fucked that all up, beyond repair and she didn't care about those she hurt.

Through my family, I met the lady that put me up on game about the tax shit.

That was Tie's friend. The lady met and fell in love with my great-grandma. She was about twenty-eight, maybe thirty-two years old.

She had a daughter and two, possibly three sons. She befriended my family. I lived in an apartment upstairs, and she lived across from me. Great-grandma lived downstairs.

We became family. She met other people in my family, and we were introduced to other members of her family.

She started fooling around with Lil Dave, one of my brother's friends. My brother started messing around with her daughter.

The tax place she hooked me up with was located right down the street in a plaza. It was within a reasonable walking distance.

I went and picked up my check and it was for $10,000. Back into the sun I went, walking to the check cashing place. The store was on the same block.

Come to think of it, I called for a ride to the check cashing store. I didn't walk there, especially with a check that size.

They wanted nearly all the money. I was left with three, maybe four thousand dollars. I second guessed my efforts. I made a decision. I wasn't giving them shit

She was the only person I ever worked with I didn't pay. I didn't pay her because I felt like they were ripping me off.

What happened was, they were supposed to do something on their end, to where they pick up the check and pay me a cut. They didn't tell me that I was getting that much. I just told them that I wanted three grand, but what they didn't tell me was how much the check was going to be.

They hid the sum from me in hopes I wouldn't catch on or find out. My ignorance in the scheme I felt they played on.

So, instead of the tax people calling them, they called me to pick up the check.

And when I saw $10,000, and they were getting about 7,000 of that, I was good.

I kept it all.

CHAPTER THIRTY-EIGHT
THE DOUBLE-CROSS

I was heated. "They got me fucked up! They are trying to pimp me like I'm new to the game."

If it was me, there was no way I'd keep all that and give my clients two or three grand. Out of $10,000?

I should have at least gotten five grand out of the deal, and y'all get the other half, since they were finessing clients before I came along. Now I had the whole ten. Double for my troubles. I was going to get mine.

Come on, now. People were greedy. I wasn't worried because they didn't get that money, nor did I give them peanuts from it, two or three grand, like they tried to give me.

Did I look stupid?

Maybe I was, because that $10,000 I blew through in a week. And I didn't buy a car.

I did pay my rent. At this time, me and my cousin fell out. There was now bad blood between us. I was there by myself, paying all the bills.

We'd been together, close, since we were kids, making and eating dirt pies. We never had an argument or a fight. We never had a falling out about anything.

Yet when I received a letter that I was approved for a two bedroom down south, in Naranja, things didn't go well. She already knew I was on a waiting list for HUD subsidized housing. I filled out the application when I was 16 years old.

Every time I moved, I made sure I informed the HUD office with my address, so I didn't miss my name when it came up.

I also called periodically to check where my name was ranked on the list. I waited four years for my chance to get a place for me and my daughter.

She also knew that when I was approved, she could live with me. That was the plan.

The letter came around my birthday. I was excited! I ran to my cousin, with joy in my heart.

"Cousin! Cousin! I have an interview down south for a two bedroom!"

At face value, she was happy, but looks could be deceiving. Later on, she stopped speaking to me. She'd walk around with her nose tooted in the air like she was better than me.

She started slamming doors around the house like she had lost her marbles. I was like, what the fuck.

She made it so uncomfortable, I went downstairs and asked my sister, and her boyfriend would they mind switching homes with me, so I could live with great-grandma. They would get my old room and I would get theirs.

I was tired of the negative energy. After we switched rooms, my sister called me, saying that my cousin wanted her to get the fuck out of her house.

Wait a minute, bitch. That wasn't just her house. First of all, my name was on the lease and her boyfriend's name was on there as well. Her name couldn't go on the lease.

Secondly, for her to be cocky like that, she did pay the security deposit, but I paid half of the bills. Was she serious?

And the money she used for the deposit was from her big time Jamaican drug-dealing baby daddy sent her from Jamaica.

At the end of the day, that was money that was given to you. You didn't earn a dime of that money. Baby daddy made sure his child had a roof, was the way I saw it. She was just an independent clause in the grand scheme of things.

In lament terms, she didn't have the legal authority to throw my sister out or tell her to get the fuck out.

So, if she wanted to walk around with an attitude then that was on her. I literally cried to the bitch. I was like, "What's wrong, cousin?"

I was boo-hoo crying terribly, and the bitch sat there, cold, with her nose tooted in the air.

"Ain't nothing wrong with me. What are you talking about?"

Things were tense after I received my approval letter for subsidized housing, and after I asked my sister to switch rooms with me, she got an attitude because she didn't want my sister there. She didn't want my sister going into the refrigerator.

Hold up. I told my sister the only items in the fridge she could touch were the things that I paid for, which was a lot. She wouldn't touch anything that belonged to my cousin.

My sister wasn't violating her shit. She was treating me like shit, keeping attitudes and bad energy when we never had a falling out.

My sister moved back with great-grandma, and I went back home. One night, when me and my daughter got home, I tried to unlock the door, but the locks had been changed.

This black, ant-looking, bucktoothed, pussy ho locked me and my baby girl out in the cold like bums seeking change.

I started knocking on the door. My baby looked confused. I was in my feelings something serious. How did you lock me out of my own shit?

"Open the door, Lynn!"

"This shit is mine! You and your baby ain't coming in here. Get the fuck away from my house!"

"Do you not know that the lease is in my name?"

"I don't give a fuck! I paid the fucking deposit."

"Yes, but I pay half of the rent, half of the light bill, half of the gas bill, and the groceries so this is our place. Furthermore, again, your name is not on the lease. If I call the police you're going to get put out."

"I don't give a fuck!"

"You're already on papers!"

"I don't have to go no motherfucking place!"

"Alright, bitch! If you think you are gonna leave me and my baby out in the street while you're chilling in an apartment with my name on it, bitch you're bold."

She still talked shit from the other side of the door.

"You better make sure that this is what you really want to do. I never did shit to you. And your boyfriend's name is also on the lease, so he doesn't have to go anywhere. And I'll walk around butt-fucking-naked, in front of him, if you try me, if you want to go there. Don't start some shit you can't finish, bitch."

"Whatever, bitch, do what you gotta to. I still don't give a fuck!"

"Okay, bitch!"

I called the police.

"9-1-1."

"Yes, I'm locked outside of my apartment, on my own property. I have the lease to prove this is my place. The person inside has illegally changed the locks without my permission or knowledge, so I can't get inside. Me and my young daughter is outside, homeless."

The police was there in no time. Okay, bitch. I told you don't start no shit you couldn't finish, now it was time to play.

A few cops approached me. "Hello, ma'am. Do you have your lease to prove this is your apartment?"

"I have it right here, sir!"

I handed it to him, and he verified the information. "Well, what's going on, ma'am?"

The bitch chimed in. "The place might be in her name, but I put down cash for the deposit."

Did you think I was going to confirm that after she locked me out of my shit, temporarily taking away my daughter's peace of mind, safety and security?

Bitch, fuck you. "No, sir! She's lying to justify changing my locks and she's not on the lease! I pay all the bills! She don't pay shit but a free ride!"

Now it was my word against hers because she wanted to be nasty and lock me and my daughter out in the street. Now I didn't give a fuck about putting her and her baby out in the street. Pussy ho!

"Oh, bitch, I paid the depos—"

"—no sir," I interrupted the bitch. "She didn't pay a dime! The dude that lives here, that's his girlfriend that was only supposed to be here for a few days, but she is stirring up shit because she has to leave. Her boyfriend is my cousin. He's on the lease, she's not. Me and my daughter went out, and we returned home to the locks changed on my door, locking us out in the streets."

He looked over the lease.

"This is me and my **boyfriend**'s apartment, sir!"

"Well, ma'am," he said to the pussy ho. "You are trespassing! You broke the law. You don't have the legal right to change the locks on a place in someone else's name!"

She snapped! The bitch was pissed! Was she mad or nah? Mind you, she was on papers from the law.

"You made this decision! You made this bed you have to sleep in," I said.

"Well, what about all my stuff in here?"

"Ma'am, that isn't your stuff. And if it is, it's a civil matter," the police told her.

"She knows this is my shit!"

"Girl, please! There's nothing in my house that belongs to you, except for the clothes on your back and your dirty laundry."

"You grimy bitch!"

"You did this. Locking me out of my apartment. Karma is a bitch! What goes around comes around. Now get your ass outta my apartment! My baby is sleepy."

The bitch was hurt. Once she left my house me and my baby were good. She had a cousin that lived in the back of the apartment. She tried to set it up where she could come with her cousin to get her stuff the next day.

Her auntie called me. "Yes."

"Shanta, now you know you and Lynn are close. Y'all are cousins! Ya'll shouldn't be going through this. I'm coming with her so she can get her stuff."

Chile, please. "Y'all ain't coming to get shit! She wanted to be nasty, locking me and my baby out of our own shit, leaving us homeless in the street.
I never did anything to her; I still don't know what I did to her or why she was tripping. She changed my locks and told me and my baby to get the fuck away? She started that nasty shit; I'm going to finish it."

I put that ho's shit outside, downstairs, by the garbage can, and called her family and told them they better come get it.

Remember, we lived in Little Haiti. I looked over the railing from my floor and those Haitians bum rushed her shit, taking whatever they could grab.

They were running with the pussy ho's shit like it was money from an armored truck that flipped over. They had chairs and all types of shit.

The only thing I gave her back was her stereo system. And I snatched the wires out of that.

When she was nasty to my daughter, there was no coming back from that. I saw her twice since then, but we were never the same. That shit was over, nipped in the bud.

When this all went down, she was bringing up shit from when we were teenagers. I was like, what the fuck. Was that how you always felt about me?

I was shocked about the shit she was bringing up.

I couldn't believe it.

It made me question were we ever close, or cool with each other. I never knew she felt that way about me.

For her to bring up that type of shit from the past, and we were grown women let me know that she been had a personal vendetta against me. There was no coming back from that.

That was when I moved down South.

Chapter Thirty-Nine
The Mortgage

My Great-grandma ended up taking a mortgage out on the house because of her situation that was televised to the general public. Once it was approved, she was able to rebuild it, but the builders did a piss poor job. That was another story.

I was talking to an older Jamaican dude I'd known since I was 15. Even when I was dating Pat, the Haitian dude that went back to his ex-fiancé, I was still talking to the Jamaican dude. The thing was the Jamaican dude didn't come at me for sex.

For the two years I was with the Haitian dude, I would stop by and see the Jamaican dude when I randomly went to Opa-Locka. He was part owner of an Auto Repair Shop.

He would give me free Jamaican food because he was always cooking and he would give me a few hundred-dollar bills, on the house, just because.

He was an older dude, and he was in love with me, but he loved me for me, not because of sex or lust.

His type of respect for women was hard to find.

There was a saying that nothing was free, but he redefined that term and showed me that there were real men out there with a genuine love for women. He was a rare breed, a rare find you didn't see in younger dudes.

One thing about it, my experience with dating older dudes was never based on sex. I would talk to an older dude for about a year, and we'd have sex probably once, maybe twice. During that whole year older dudes would make sure that I was taken care of. I didn't want for anything.

That was why I always dated older dudes because they weren't worried about fucking me all the time. The average dude I always dated were older and mature.

I'd never met an older dude that just wanted to fuck, fuck, fuck. They took the time to get to know me. They made me smile when I came around.

It was the younger dudes, the ones that were a little older than me, that just wanted to fuck, fuck, fuck all the time. Didn't give a damn about getting to know you. They'd promise you anything just to fuck. Once it was over, they chased other hos.

But the older dudes, the ones that were around my daddy's age, didn't treat me like that.

With that being said, the Jamaican dude helped me move down south to my new place. I was happy that me and my daughter officially had our own space.

We no longer had to worry about a pussy ho changing our locks. We didn't have to worry about being homeless.

A huge weight was lifted off my shoulders. Jamaican dude rented me a U-haul truck and all. No questions asked. He had my phone turned on, my utilities turned on, all that. I didn't have to pay for shit or get on my back and shake a little something.

I was grateful and very appreciative. The pussy ho changed the locks and told me and my baby to get the fuck away, but Jamaican dude made sure I moved into my place with no thought of homelessness.

Now I lived down south. It was 1998. I was still dabbling in schemes. I was done with income tax shit; I was just filing. I inevitably gravitated towards bank fraud, my new scheme.

As far as the Jamaican dude was concerned, I guessed our friendship ran its course. When he rented me the U-Haul, I drove that bitch between Opa-Locka and down south like it was a regular car.

He had put $250 down for me to get the truck, and when we took the truck back, he had a $400 (+) bill to pay.

Then he gave me a Nissan Maxima car to drive around. I could just get in and go wherever I wanted to go. I let my sister Tie and her friends, who were my friends, too, hold the car to go around the corner and come right back. Shit, they had the man's car for three, maybe four days.

I kept telling him to call the police on her ass, but he wouldn't do it. He refused. Tie and her friends were having a grand ole time.

Tie was putting the pedal to the medal. The bitch was zooming all through The City, Opa-Locka,

Carol City. Every place I searched for then they had just left, or I'd just missed them.

Tie made it hard for me and the Jamaican dude was taking care of me and my daughter. There was so much evil shit she did to me. I was surprised I still picked up the phone when she called me. If I had half a brain I'd cut her ass completely off, especially since she never admitted or acknowledged her wrongdoings, but she was still my sister, blood.

After the car situation, the Jamaican dude faded away. We slowly went our own way. I didn't know how I met the white dude, Manny.

He was the dude that knocked on my door, saying that he worked for the insurance company, and he wanted to know what kind of plan I had.

He was flirting with me. He came back a few times and we exchanged numbers, and a new scheming opportunity came into play.

Since he worked at an insurance company, he had access to people's records and their information. He'd give me stacks of paper and I'd act like I was the client and put them back on the insurance.

These people have been clients, didn't like it and left. He would have me pretending to be an agent, call, and add them back on.

Once he added them back on to the insurance plan, it didn't matter because he still received commission. They could cancel again, didn't matter. That commission was guaranteed.

I was getting paid so many dollars for each child and each person on the cases that I did. That was extra money. Plus, he started paying my bills.

One of my friends out of the Hound Pound put me up on the bank fraud scheme. I learned how to flip checks and put fake money into bank accounts.

I learned fast. I used blank checks from closed accounts. When the weekend came, I wrote a lot of checks to the same bank in different locations and put them in the drop box.

By 12 midnight the system would show the sum of all those checks. Then I hit every ATM over the weekend getting all the cash out before business hours on Monday.

It was really popular in the 90s. With all that new game, I took it and ran with it. I didn't blow up from it, but it brought me some good money. A lot of people didn't care about fucking up their credit. You could get thousands and go shopping?

Around this time, I met the man who would wind up being my fiancé, Clinton Lidell Young. . We played around with each other for two years. We'd randomly called each other, but nothing too serious. We never hung out with each other.

We finally got together in 2000. After talking and playing around, plus he had a girlfriend at the time. Once I got with him, I was still doing the bank fraud shit, but that slowly faded after nearly two years.

When I got with my new boyfriend, it was a wrap. I couldn't go clubbing, I couldn't wear color hair, I had to go to school. I didn't complain.

I completely gave up the bank shit. Business dried up anyway, the thrill was gone. Everyone was hip to it.

Everybody started flipping checks and fucking it up. Banks started getting strict to curb the wave of fraud.

Bank fraud was the last level of scheming I'd ever done, and it ended after bank fraud. Believe it or not, after that I went to work, besides helping my fiancé with his business.

I didn't have to work, but I chose to. And it felt good to make my own money without robbing, scheming, stripping, purse snatching or bank fraud.

Talk about good times. I remember we went to Marathon, in The Florida Keys. I was about 21 years old, maybe 22. We were going to rent jet skis.

When we arrived, we needed a credit card to rent it, but we didn't have one.

We had a lot of expensive jewelry, so we let the owner of the Shop hold two expensive Cuban links with the diamond pendants as collateral and we were able to have fun on one.

We had a ball. We made a way out of no way. I had never ridden on a jet ski with someone. I always rode a jet ski by myself, but to share it with him was special.

We were laughing, having fun under the sun...

EPILOGUE

To me, my great grandma Patsy was my Mama. She was a very big blessing in my life, so was my Pa-Pa.

She died at the 102 years old. I was 38 years old when she passed away, and I was a grandmother.

My daughter had a daughter by that time, and my great-grandma was able to meet her.

It was like she gave up on life in 2015. She stopped eating.

Worried, I went to visit her in Opa-locka. I sat in her bedroom with her, in shambles.

"Great-Grandma, please! I'm not ready for you to leave! I can't do this by myself."

She said, "Ok I'll eat."

The following year she stopped eating again. And when I asked her, she said that she couldn't do it again for me because she was tired.

I was so angry because I felt like when she left me that was all I really had.

Somebody that raised me, that I knew besides my Pa-Pa and my dad's mother.

They all raised me.